GARDENERS' WORLD

INSTANT GARDENING

GARDENERS' WORLD

INSTANT GARDENING

25 Quick & Easy Projects to
Transform your Garden

Gay Search

BBC BOOKS

Acknowledgements

Grateful thanks are due to all the designers involved in these projects, not just for their talent but for their tolerance and enthusiasm, and to Amanda Lowe and James Ebdon for some bright ideas. I am particularly grateful to Jean Goldberry, Penny Smith and Louise and Learie Hampden who worked with me in all weathers, and sometimes in very difficult conditions, to get the projects done and to Tony, as always, for moral support and deft wielding of the Deep Heat.

Other BBC Books in the Gardeners' World series:
Gardeners' World Perfect Plants for Problem Places by Gay Search
Gardeners' World Book of Water Gardens by Sue Fisher
Gardeners' World Book of Container Gardening by Anne Swithinbank

Published by BBC Books
an imprint of BBC Worldwide Publishing,
BBC Worldwide Ltd,
Woodlands, 80 Wood Lane
London W12 0TT

First published 1995

© Gay Search 1995

ISBN: 0 563 37075 0

Designed by Andrew Shoolbred
Photographs by Anne Hyde
Small 'before' photographs on pages 14, 23, 35 and 93 by William Shaw
Plans by Jane Craddock-Watson

Set in Bembo by Ace Filmsetting Ltd, Frome
Printed and bound in Great Britain by Butler & Tanner Ltd, Frome
Colour separation by Radstock Reproductions Ltd, Midsomer Norton
Cover printed by Clays Ltd, St Ives plc

Contents

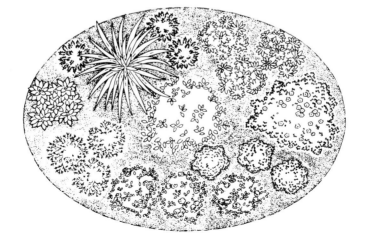

Introduction

There's no doubt that, where gardening is concerned, nothing succeeds – or inspires – like success, and that's especially true for beginners. There is nothing quite like the thrill of watching your first packet of seeds germinate, or seeing that small group of shrubs and perennials which you planted last spring actually looking wonderful, their colours, their overall shape, their foliage blending together and complementing each other in a way that gives you pleasure every time you look at them.

It's also true that nothing deflates like failure. So many new gardeners rush off to the garden centre with a great deal of enthusiasm and an open cheque book to load up the trolley with lots of plants that catch their eye, but without any idea of where they're going to plant them. Then they get them home and put them in the borders, only to find the end result disappointing in the extreme. Either the plants don't thrive because the conditions aren't right for them, or, because they've just been dotted about the garden, they have no impact at all and don't add up to anything very much. Not surprisingly people conclude either that gardening is very difficult or that it isn't for them, which is such a shame since it is one of the most delightful pastimes there is, one that could last you several lifetimes, and the best form of therapy I've come across.

So this book, aimed at new gardeners of any age, sets out to help you succeed by taking you step by step through a number of small-scale planting projects and showing you exactly what you'll get at the end of each one. Since most of them rely primarily for their effect on the choice of plants and the combinations in which they are used together, we have asked some of the country's best garden designers to dream up these schemes for you.

Each project starts off with the ingredients – exactly which plants you'll need and how many of each, which sundries (a lovely old nurseryman's word, that) like compost, soil improver, fertilizer, mulch, pots and so forth, and what tools you'll require to do the job.

Given how busy most people's lives are these days, all the projects can be done in a day – from start to finish. Promise! Very occasionally the 'day' needs to be spread over two days because you'll have to leave cement to set or stain to dry. In one or two cases there's a little very simple construction involved, but don't panic! The most sophisticated tools you're ever going to need are a screwdriver, a hammer, an electric drill and an extra pair of hands. For a couple of projects you'll need a very early start, though of course you could buy your ingredients the day before and there is nothing to stop you taking more than a day if you want to. Other projects, however, which consist more or less exclusively of planting, can be completed in a morning or an afternoon and at a fairly leisurely pace, complete with tea breaks and a chance to stand back and admire what you've done.

The time each project takes, particularly those that involve digging out an area first, will depend entirely on what your soil is like. If it is really heavy clay, digging it will take much longer – twice as long or even more – than it would if the soil was light and sandy. The times I've given are those for an average soil, so you'll need to adjust them up or down according to the conditions in your garden. Do take it easy, especially if you have a heavy soil and a fair bit of digging over to do. If you rush things, you could hurt your back and wear yourself out, which is guaranteed to take the shine off anyone's enthusiasm. I haven't included tea breaks in every recipe, but they are allowed for, and you should take them. It really is 'tortoise and hare' – you'll find that if you work for a bit and rest for a bit, you'll get there just as fast if not faster, and certainly in better shape than you will if you go at it furiously and wear yourself out. After all, this is fun!

The choice of plants is the key to success with all these projects, but if we'd confined ourselves to those which are guaranteed to be available in every single garden centre, no matter how small, or street market or local greengrocer's, we'd have had a very limited range of plants to draw on and I think that would have been a great shame. Equally there would be no point in using an absolutely stunning plant if it's available only from a small specialist nursery in a remote Highland village, needs a very acid soil, precisely the right amount of shade and there's a three-year waiting list for it anyway. So you should be able to get almost all the plants we've used from a good, well-stocked garden centre, and remember that most will order particular plants for you if they don't have them in stock. Some plants, like palms, for example, you can buy yourself by mail order. I know that means you won't be able to do the project this instant, but waiting a week or two won't make a lot of difference, will it?

Now for the thorny question of plant names. I know that lots of new gardeners see a Latin name and run a mile. While there is no point in calling a rose *'Rosa'* or rosemary *'Rosmarinus'* because it's perfectly clear what we're all talking about, in many instances giving a plant its proper botanical name is the only way of making sure that you get the right one when you go to buy it. And since most garden centres group plants under their proper names and in alphabetical order, it makes shopping less frustrating and tiring too. People often ask why we can't use common names, but the problem with those is that, in many instances, they are not all that common. One book on British wildflowers lists over one hundred different 'common' names for the same plant! What might be bachelor's buttons in one part of the country will be granny's bonnets somewhere else and nanny's nightcaps somewhere else again. Not only can one plant have lots of different common names, but, even more confusingly, sometimes different plants share the same common name. Take burning bush – that can be *Dictamnus fraxinella* or *D. albus*, a tall, branching, perennial plant with small, scented, purple or white flowers which give off a vapour in the evenings which can be ignited, so it really is a burning bush or it can be *Kochia scoparia*, an annual grown for its foliage, which looks like a bright green guardsman's busby in summer and turns vivid red in autumn, so it really looks like a burning bush. Now obviously it will make a huge difference to your planting scheme if you get the wrong one. So I have listed each plant under its common name – if it has one that really is common – with its proper name alongside. It seems to me that if you are a new gardener, you won't have come across quite a lot of the plants we're using before, so it's just as easy to learn their proper names as the common ones. Honest!

While there are different schemes to take account of different aspects, sun and shade, we have tended to use plants that are happy in the average soil – one that isn't too acid, too alkaline, too wet and sticky, or too thin and free-draining. At the end of the book there is a chapter on techniques, which includes a section on improving your soil, so if yours is very heavy clay or very free-draining, for instance, you can see how to improve it to make it more hospitable for the plants you want to grow.

While each project is laid out in precise detail, like a recipe, that doesn't mean you have to follow it to the letter if you don't want to. Take from it what you want and ignore the rest. If you want to use different plants or different colours, that's terrific. It's your garden, after all, and the only thing that matters is that you like it. The last thing I want to do is stifle creativity or individuality, or impose my own tastes on anyone. But I am convinced, after talking to many novice gardeners over the years, that what most of them want to do is to create an attractive garden, somewhere pleasurable to be, and what many of them find extremely difficult is knowing how to combine plants in a way that looks good.

For trees, shrubs and perennials I have given an approximate height and spread, but of course there can be considerable variation according to the conditions in which they are grown. For annuals, used in containers or to infill, there's no point in giving the height and spread since they're there for only one season. The same is true of vegetables, because as soon as they are big enough you eat them! In general, we have planted everything a bit closer together than most books recommend. I take the view that with projects like these, it's better to get results in a year or two, and be prepared to take out a few plants in three or four years' time when the bed becomes overcrowded, than to plant at the correct distances and wait four or five years to get the effect.

What these projects can do is give you a bit of guaranteed success, the chance to draw directly on the experience and the 'eye' of some of the best designers around and apply them in your own garden. By actually doing the planting for yourself and getting your hands dirty, you will have the chance to learn at first hand why that particular combination of plants works so well – the blend or contrast of colours, of leaf shapes and textures, and so on. Then, armed with that knowledge and buoyed up with the glow of success, you will feel confident enough to try something of your own next time. So go on, have a go!

Out front – Japanese style

〜

DESIGNER

Judith Sharp

Many houses built since the 1960s have very small front gardens, often not much more than a little patch of lawn that barely justifies carting the mower round from the back once a week to cut it. The owners of the front garden we tackled both worked full-time and had a growing family, so there was little time for gardening. What they wanted was a garden that looked more attractive than the fat, back-to-front L-shaped patch of scrubby grass they had and one that would take care of itself. The garden was 3 × 4 m (10 × 13 ft) at the outside, faced west, sloped slightly down to the house, and was bordered on all sides by pavement, paths or driveway.

A Japanese-style garden, mainly gravel with just a few 'architectural' plants – those grown for their overall shape and the bold shape of their leaves – some larger pebbles and a few very large boulders seemed the perfect solution, especially with a layer of woven membrane laid underneath the gravel to keep water in, suppress weeds and prevent local cats from using it as a litter tray.

At its best in spring when the bergenias and euphorbias flower and the new leaves open on the rhus, and autumn when the latter's leaves turn red, but designed to look good all year.

—— Plants ——

Stag's Horn Sumach (Rhus typhina)
Height/spread in 10 years: 4 × 4 m (13 × 13 ft) but can be pruned

3 Euphorbia characias
Height/spread: 80 × 80 cm (32 × 32 in)

8 Elephant's Ears (Bergenia) 'Sunningdale'
Height/spread: 30 × 30 cm (12 × 12 in)

—— Sundries ——

Soil improver
Pelleted chicken manure or slow-release fertilizer
12 sq m (130 sq ft) Plantex weed-control membrane

12 25 kg (55 lb) bags pea gravel – 1 bag per sq m (11 sq ft)
2 25 kg (55 lb) sacks small mixed pebbles
3 large boulders

The following July the garden is looking very good. Although the *bergenias* have finished flowering, their lovely, round evergreen leaves more than justify their place in the garden.

—— Tools ——

Hose or watering can
Wheelbarrow or groundsheet
Spade
Trowel
Garden knife
Heavy-duty scissors
Bucket or large empty
flowerpot

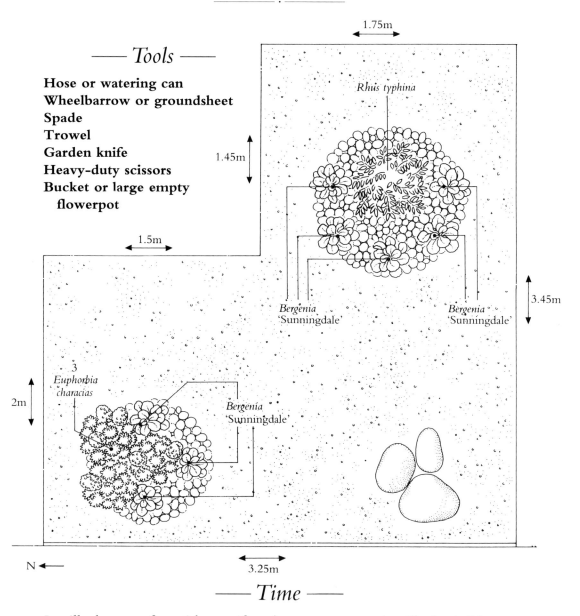

1.75m

Rhus typhina

1.45m

1.5m

3.45m

Bergenia
'Sunningdale'

Bergenia
'Sunningdale'

3
Euphorbia
characias

Bergenia
'Sunningdale'

2m

N ←

3.25m

—— Time ——

It will take two of you 3 hours; if you're on your own, it will take 4–5 hours. The longest job is digging.

—— Method ——

1. Give all the plants a thorough watering.

2. Get rid of the grass by digging it out, taking a few centimetres of soil with it. You will be spreading a couple of centimetres of gravel in its place once the plants are in, and you want this to come to just below the surrounding hard surfaces to keep it in place.

3. Dig over the two main areas in which you will be planting, and improve the soil. (If yours is a very heavy clay soil, you'll need to dig a much wider area, otherwise your planting holes will just act as a sump. See page 116.)

4. Cut the planting membrane to size with scissors and lay it in strips to cover the soil, overlapping it by 7.5–10 cm (3–4 in) where it joins and leaving 7.5–10 cm (3–4 in) around the edges.

5. Set out the plants, still in their pots, on the membrane and adjust them until you're happy with the way they look.

6. To plant, cut large Xs in the membrane with a sharp knife, fold under the corners, and dig out the soil with a trowel, putting the surplus into a bucket or large flowerpot. Plant in the usual way (see page 117), then pull out the corners of the membrane to fit snugly round the stem. With trees or large shrubs, especially if they're quite close to the edge of the planting membrane, it's easier to roll it back, dig out the hole with a spade, plant, and then cut the membrane from the edge to fit round the plant. The only drawback is that the more cuts there are in the membrane, the greater the chance of weeds finding their way through. If the soil is dry, water around the planted areas (the membrane is water-permeable).

7. Lay the pebbles in broad curves in front of each group of bergenias, and place the three large boulders in the most attractive arrangement you can come up with. Handle the boulders with care – they will be heavy and can damage fingers or toes. Then spread the gravel over the rest of the garden. Because the membrane will suppress weeds and keep moisture in, the gravel is purely ornamental, and so needs be only a couple of centimetres deep or even less. That not only keeps the costs down but discourages cats since they quickly catch the membrane with their claws as they start to dig.

Magic! The shed has disappeared. In another year's time,
even less of the trellis will be visible as the climbers fill out.

Hiding the shed

~

DESIGNER

Jacqui Stubbs

Most of us need a shed of some kind to store all the essentials for gardening – the tools, the compost, the fertilizers and so on. But in small gardens they can take up a disproportionate amount of space, and even when they are tucked away in a corner – in our case, in the angle between a well-trimmed leylandii hedge and the fence – they still have a tendency to stick out like a sore thumb. The object of this project is to hide the shed and assorted necessary but unattractive bits of kit, like incinerators and compost heaps, and at the same time make an attractive feature in the garden with off-the-peg trellis panels, wood stain and some colourful climbing plants. This is a project that really does require an early start (or better still get the local builders' merchant to deliver the trellis panels, posts and post supports the day before) and an extra pair of hands – preferably large competent ones on the end of fairly muscular arms!

At its best from April to October/November, starting with the *Clematis alpina* in April, followed by the roses, the other clematis and the solanum flowering all summer, and the autumn colour of the Virginia creeper. The ivy will look good all year.

—— *Plants* ——

1 **Virginia creeper (*Parthenocissus henryana*)**
Height/spread after 10 years: 5×3 m (16×10 ft)

1 **Rose (*Rosa* 'Golden Showers')**
Height/spread after 10 years: 3 × 3 m (10 × 10 ft)

1 **Rose (*Rosa* 'New Dawn')**
Height/spread after 10 years: 3 × 3 m (10 × 10 ft)

1 ***Clematis* 'Perle d'Azur'**
Height/spread after 10 years: 3–4 × 3–4 m (10–13 × 10–13 ft)

1 ***Clematis alpina* 'Frances Rivis'**
Height/spread after 10 years: 3 × 3 m (10 × 10 ft)

1 ***Clematis* 'Hagley Hybrid'**
Height/spread after 10 years: 3–4 × 3–4 m (10–13 × 10–13 ft)

1 ***Clematis* 'Duchess of Albany'**
Height/spread after 10 years: 3 × 3 m (10 × 10 ft)

1 ***Solanum jasminoïdes* 'Album'**
Height/spread after 10 years: 4 × 4 m (13 × 13 ft)

1 **Persian ivy (*Hedera colchica* 'Dentata Variegata')**
Height/spread after 10 years: 4 × 4 m (13 × 13 ft)

3 **trays of bedding plants**
(To tone with the roses and climbers)

— Sundries —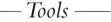

6 panels 1.8 × 1 m (6 × 3 ft)
squared trellis panels

8 treated posts 2.4 × 75 mm ×
75 mm (8 ft × 3 in × 3 in)

8 post caps

8 spiked 75 × 75 mm (3 × 3 in)
Metposts (plus dolly for driving
them into the soil)

50 5 cm (2 in) galvanized nails
litre wood stain (we used
Hickson's Decor Wood Stain in
'Neptune')

Soil improver

Pelleted chicken manure or slow-
release fertilizer

Soft garden twine

— Tools —

Hose or watering can

Tape measure

Pegs or skewers

Long metal spike

Sledge hammer (you can hire
one if you don't own one)

Step ladder

Hammer

Bradawl

Spirit level

Paint brushes

Stout gloves

Spade

Trowel

Garden knife

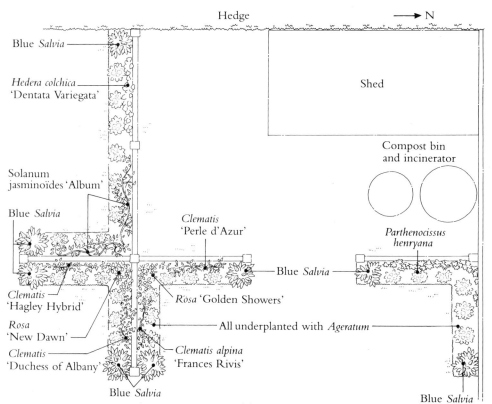

—— Time ——

It will take two of you 6–8 hours, and it really is something you can't do single-handed. That does *not* include waiting time for two coats of wood stain to dry, so you can do the planting, which won't take more than an hour, on the following day.

—— Method ——

1. Give all the plants a thorough watering.

2. Using a tape measure and a peg or skewer, measure and mark out the position for the central post on to which four trellis panels will be fixed, since that dictates the position for everything else. Make a hole for the Metpost for the central post using the long metal spike. That way you will find out if there is any obstruction under the soil which could damage the Metpost when you drive it in, and it also makes the job easier. Using the dolly provided, drive the first Metpost into the ground, making sure it doesn't twist in the process.

3. Once that is securely fixed, put the first post into the hole, wearing gloves to avoid splinters. Then, while one of you holds it steady, the other climbs up the step ladder and, having slipped the dolly over the end of the post to stop the wood splitting, hammers the post firmly into the Metpost. Check regularly with a spirit level on the front or back, and on one side, to check that the post is going in straight in both planes – forward and backward and side to side.

4. When the first post is in securely and straight, attach the first trellis panel to it. You might think that the simplest way of tackling this job is to put all the posts in first and then fix the trellis panels to them. But you've only got to be a centimetre or so out with a post, either too near or too far away, to give yourself a major problem, since trellis panels won't stretch or scrunch up to fit. It's much safer to fit panel to post, then post to panel.

5. Use a spare fence post laid on the ground to support the weight of the panel at the right height while you nail through the panel into the post. Make a small hole for each nail first with a bradawl, which will help prevent the wood splitting. Six nails each 30 cm (1 ft) apart should hold it.

6. Put in the next Metpost right by the end of the first panel, making sure that it is exactly in line with the central post. Carry on until all four posts and panels are in, as well as the additional panel to complete the one long side. With the last single panel, put the post closest to the boundary in first. Since this panel adjoins the entrance to the utility area, it doesn't matter whether the entrance is actually a few centimetres wider or narrower than it is on the plan. Nail the caps in place on the posts.

7. Stain everything with wood stain. Leave for at least 6 hours to dry and then give it another coat.

8. When the stain on the trellis is dry, dig out narrow curved beds in the right-angled bays created by the four-way trellis panels and straight ones along the rest. Improve the soil (see page 116), and plant as usual (see page 117). Remember to plant all clematis 10–15 cm (4–6 in) deeper than they are in their pots (see page 119).

9. Spread the stems of the roses as horizontally as you can – that way you encourage them to produce more side shoots which will grow up and in turn produce more flowers – and tie them to the trellis with soft garden twine. Tuck the young growths of the solanum through the trellis while they are still flexible. The clematis will cling on by its leaf stalks once it starts growing, so weave existing growth in and out of the trellis to get it started. The Virginia creeper and the ivy are both self-clinging when they start producing new growth, but to get them started weave the existing shoots through the trellis in the same way.

10. Plant the bedding plants in front of the climbers. They will shade the roots of the clematis from the sun, and that's how clematis do best. Since permanent climbers and temporary bedding will be competing for food and water, make sure that you water regularly – every day if it's hot – and feed once a week with a liquid all-purpose fertilizer.

Grass with a difference

~

DESIGNER

Penelope Smith

Very small areas of lawn, especially those in front gardens, rarely look good, partly because they need such a lot of attention to keep them at their best, and for most people it's just too much hassle to cart the mower round to the front a couple of times a week in the growing season. Ornamental grasses, though, are an entirely different matter. Many are evergreen, look very attractive and, apart from an annual trim to remove the dead flowering stalks in winter (or even in the spring, since frost on the dead flower heads looks really lovely), they don't need very much attention.

The waist-high ground elder and docks concealed a pretty layout, within which the pattern of grasses works well.

19

The garden we chose for this project, in front of a small 1920s semi, had a rectangular bed – 1.2 × 1.8 m (4 × 6 ft) – in the centre, with a broad path of crazy paving surrounding it. The garden faced north-west, so got some sun in summer, particularly in the latter part of the day. The soil tended towards clay, though not too heavy, and so we improved it by digging in gravel and compost to make it more free-draining, since that's what ornamental grasses need.

We decided to adapt a style of carpet bedding beloved of Victorians and latterly of public parks, but making patterns with ornamental grasses instead. Obviously, if your space isn't exactly the same as this one, draw it out to scale on graph paper and then create any design you like. You will need roughly twenty plants per sq m (11 sq ft), though it's well worth setting the design out at the garden centre when you go to buy your grasses with the plants still in their pots, and making any adjustments then. Tell the staff what you're going to do first, or they may think you have flipped!

At its best all year round.

—— *Plants* ——

48 *Festuca eskia*
Height/spread after 10 years: 15 × 22 cm (6 × 9 in)

16 *Carex berggrenii*
Height/spread after 10 years: 10–15 × 22 cm (4–6 × 9 in)

5 *Carex oshimensis* 'Evergold'
Height/spread after 10 years: 20 × 20 cm (8 × 8 in)

—— *Sundries* ——

Soil improver
Pelleted chicken manure or slow-release fertilizer

—— *Tools* ——

Hose or watering can
Spade
Fork
Trowel

—— *Time* ——

It will take two people about 2 hours; one person about 3 hours.

—— *Method* ——

1. Give all the plants a thorough watering.

2. Dig over the bed, improving the soil if you need to (see page 116).

3. Set out the plants, still in their pots, on the soil, and make any adjustments to the positioning then. Make sure that the central plant in the design is absolutely dead centre, then remove the ring of plants immediately around it to give yourself room to work, and plant it with a trowel.

4. Plant the immediately surrounding plants. Having set the centre of the design, start at one edge and plant the first row. Carry on planting row by row until you reach the centre, making any adjustments to the spacing as you go. Then start at another side, and again, plant row by row to the middle. Finish off the design in the same way.

5. If your bed is so wide that you can't reach the centre from the surrounding paths or lawn, either plant more of the central section first, while you can still tread on the soil, or support a plank on two upturned buckets, one each side of the bed, and work, kneeling, from that.

2m

'Evergold'

'Evergold'

1m 40

16 Carex
berggrenii

Carex
berggrenii

'Evergold'

'Evergold'

48
Festuca
eskia

Carex oshimensis 'Evergold'

21

Bed for winter colour

~

DESIGNER

Judith Sharp

While it's lovely to see colour in the garden in summer, it's almost more important in the gloomy depths of winter when otherwise the predominant colour is brown – bare brown twigs, bare brown soil, the few remaining dead brown leaves – and your spirits really can do with a lift. If you are going to plant up a bed with winter colour in mind, where you site it is almost as important as what you plant. Since most of us don't spend a great deal of time actually out in the garden in winter, you need to plant it where you're going to see it and enjoy it from the house. The site we chose for our winter bed was what the owners looked at from their living-room window – a shady corner at the bottom of the garden, facing north, with a conifer hedge on one side and a low wall covered with a rather straggly honeysuckle from the neighbouring garden on the other. The need for colour in winter meant a fair proportion of evergreens, while the position dictated the need for plants that thrive in shade, and the fact that the conifer hedge sucked most of the goodness and moisture out of the soil meant that they had to be able to cope with dry shade as well. All the plants with the exception of the cornus are evergreen, but that has lovely scarlet bark in winter to add a splash of a different colour, and cool green-and-cream-variegated leaves in spring and summer, adding much-needed lightness to the shady border then.

At its best, as planned, in winter/early spring when all the flowering shrubs and perennials (both marked F in the list below) and bulbs are in flower, though with so much evergreen foliage it's attractive all year round.

The different textures of these mainly evergreen plants mean that the bed looks good all year round, and in winter, the bright sealing-wax red stems of the dogwood (centre), after the leaves have fallen, will add a splash of winter warmth.

Plants

1 *Mahonia japonica* **F**
Height/spread after 10 years: 2.4 × 2.7 m
(8 × 9 ft)

1 False castor oil plant (*Fatsia japonica***)**
Height/spread after 10 years: 2 × 2 m (6½ × 6½ ft)

1 *Viburnum tinus* **'Gwenllian' F**
Height/spread after 10 years: 2 × 2 m (6½ × 6½ ft)

1 Dogwood (*Cornus alba* **'Elegantissima')**
Height/spread if pruned hard each year 1.5 × 1.5 m (5 × 5 ft)

1 Christmas box (*Sarcococca humilis***) F**
Height/spread after 10 years: 50 × 40 cm (20 × 16 in)

3 *Euonymus fortunei* **'Emerald Gaiety'**
Height/spread after 10 years: 60 cm × 2 m (2 × 6½ ft)

6 Christmas roses (*Helleborus niger***) F**
Height/spread: 30 × 40 cm (1 ft × 16 in)

3 Elephant's ears (*Bergenia* **'Bressingham White') F**
Height/spread: 30 × 30 cm (1 × 1 ft)

5 *Euphorbia robbiae* **F**
Height/spread: 60 × 60 cm (2 × 2 ft)

TO PLANT IN AUTUMN
Spring-flowering bulbs in white, blue and gold – small crocuses, *Anemone blanda*, dwarf daffodils, scillas and so on.

Sundries

Soil improver
Pelleted chicken manure or slow-release fertilizer

Composted bark or cocoa shells

Tools

Hose or watering can
Tape measure
Pegs or skewers
Rope (washing line or hose will do)

Spade
Fork
Wheelbarrow or ground sheet

Time

It will take two people 2–3 hours; one person 3–4 hours. The longest job is digging.

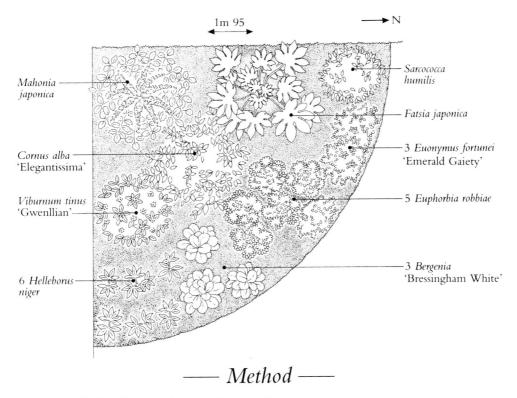

1m 95

→ N

Mahonia
japonica

Sarcococca
humilis

Fatsia japonica

Cornus alba
'Elegantissima'

3 Euonymus fortunei
'Emerald Gaiety'

Viburnum tinus
'Gwenllian'

5 Euphorbia robbiae

3 Bergenia
'Bressingham White'

6 Helleborus
niger

—— *Method* ——

1. Give all the plants a thorough watering.

2. Measure and mark out the bed with pegs or skewers and rope, and then dig it out. Improve the soil (see page 116). Set out all the plants in their pots and play with the arrangement. Ideally get someone else to stand at the window from which you're going to be looking at the bed most often and advise you on what looks best. You may find that it looks good close to, but from the house one key plant is directly screening another. When you're happy with the arrangement, plant in the usual way (see page 117), starting in the corner and working your way out.

3. When all the plants are in, water them well, and then mulch with composted bark or cocoa shells.

4. In the autumn plant spring-flowering bulbs in among the shrubs and perennials. Plant them in as generous drifts as you can afford – one clump of, say, thirty 'Tête à Tête' dwarf daffodils or white *Anemone blanda* has far greater impact than six groups of five different species, especially from a distance.

Mini jungle

~

DESIGNER

Myles Challis

Many city dwellers have only a tiny back yard or basement in which to garden and the combination of very limited space, a concrete floor and brick walls can appear quite daunting, yet it's in just such an unpromising situation that even a little bit of greenery can make a huge amount of difference. And to look on the bright side, a site like this has several pluses too. Because it's so small you need only a few plants to make a big impact, and since you need so few you can afford to splash out on some large ones. It's also likely to be sheltered, and all that brickwork surrounding it acts like a storage heater, taking in heat from the sun during the day and releasing it at night, keeping the temperature a few degrees higher than it would otherwise be, allowing you to grow plants that might not be as reliably hardy in large exposed gardens.

These factors suggest a mini jungle, a collection of exotic-looking, architectural foliage plants, like bamboos, phormiums and palms, as well as common garden plants like hostas and bear's breeches (*Acanthus mollis*) whose wonderfully dramatic leaves take on an exotic look in this context. The hosta will die back in winter, but in a sheltered situation like this the acanthus will probably keep its leaves, and all the other plants are evergreen. The contrasting shapes of the leaves not only look stunning themselves against brick walls, but cast wonderful shadows as well.

Our basement well was very small – 3 × 4 m (10 × 13 ft) – and was visible not just from the basement windows, but also from above. It faced south and so got quite a bit of sun, and the owners had already painted the walls white – an excellent way of increasing the amount of light down there.

Since the floor was concrete we chose to plant in containers, and instead of traditional terracotta or wood, we used Terraperma, an excellent new range of plastic imitation terracotta, which is totally frost-resistant, a fraction of the weight (very useful for balcony or roof gardening) and of the price.

At its best all year round.

The contrasts between the leaf shapes of these dramatic architectural
plants and the shadows they cast on the bare white walls,
brings this rather stark basement to life immediately.

—— Plants ——

1 Chusan palm (*Trachycarpus fortunei*)

Height/spread after 10 years: 3 × 2 m (10 × 6½ ft)

As a smaller alternative try *Chamaerops humilis*

Height/spread after 10 years: 1.5 × 1.5 m (5 × 5 ft)

1 Bamboo (*Fargesia nitida* – still often sold as *Arundinaria nitida*)

Height/spread after 10 years: 2.4 m (8 ft) × infinite

1 *Phormium tenax* 'Purpureum'

Height/spread after 10 years: 1.5 × 2 m (5 × 6½ ft)

1 *Hosta sieboldiana* 'Elegans'

Height/spread: 1 × 1 m (3 × 3 ft)

1 Bear's breeches (*Acanthus mollis*)

Height/spread: 1.2 m × 60 cm (4 × 2 ft)

—— Sundries ——

Terraperma pots
1 60 cm (24 in) traditional pot
1 50 cm (20 in) traditional pot
1 43 cm (17 in) traditional pot
1 50 cm (20 in) bell pot
1 35 cm (14 in) bell pot
80 litres soil-based compost

Broken polystyrene plant trays or packaging (for crocking)
16 Osmacote slow-release fertilizer plugs
1 packet Erin water-retaining gel crystals

—— Tools ——

Hose or watering can
Trowel

Garden knife
Electric drill

—— Time ——

It should take two of you less than an hour; one of you about 1½ hours.

—— Method ——

1. Give all the plants a thorough watering.

2. Drill half a dozen drainage holes in the bottom of each pot using the largest bit you have. Holes 1 cm (¼ inch) are ideal.

3. Break up the polystyrene into hand-sized chunks and put a layer over the bottom of each pot.

4. Part-fill each pot with compost, add a measure of water-retaining gel crystals and mix well with your hand.

5. Place each plant, still in its pot, in the larger pots to check the depth of compost you'll need to put in. You want to allow a gap of at least 3–4 cm (1¼–1½ in) at the top of the pot so that you can water without splashing. If the compost is too high, scoop it out to make a hollow in the centre. If it's too low, add a bit more.

6. Take each plant out of its own pot, tease out the roots if necessary and put it in position. Fill in around the sides with compost, adding a few more water-retaining gel crystals as you go. Push Osmacote plugs into the compost – four for each larger pot, three for each smaller one, evenly distributed around the rim.

7. Water well.

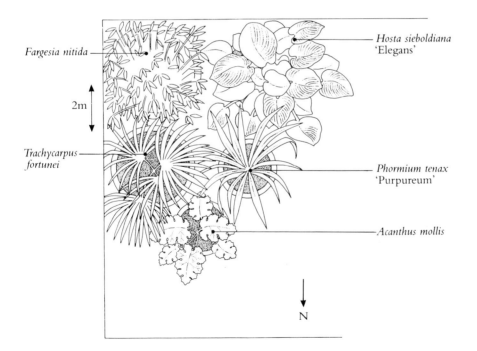

Colourful corner

~

DESIGNER

Judith Sharp

Lots of houses built in the last thirty years have open-plan front gardens with no boundaries, either real or psychological, to separate private space (the garden) from public space (the pavement). In the garden we tackled, we created a small corner bed, across the right angle formed by the drive and the pavement, which gave definition and some welcome height in the otherwise flat landscape, and also stopped local children riding their bikes across it! The house faced south, and the soil was light and gravelly, so we chose plants that like a sunny spot and a free-draining soil. The paviours of the relatively new drive were a pinky-grey, which dictated the colour scheme of the planting.

At its best from spring, when the viburnum flowers, to late summer, when the abelia finishes flowering; though as there are plenty of evergreens, it will look good all year.

—— *Plants* ——

1 *Viburnum plicatum* **'Pink Beauty'**
Height/spread after 10 years: 2.4 × 2 m (8 × 6½ ft)

1 *Abelia × grandiflora*
Height/spread after 10 years: 1.5 × 1.5 m (5 × 5 ft)

3 small or 1 large *Phormium tenax* **'Sundowner' (or 'Maori Sunrise')**
Height/spread after 10 years: 1.2 × 1.5 m (4 × 5 ft)

3 *Heuchera micrantha* **'Palace Purple'**
Height/spread: 60 × 50 cm (2 ft × 20 in)

4 *Hebe pinguifolia* **'Pagei'**
Height/spread: 30 × 80 cm (1 × 2½ ft)

Although this small corner bed is still far from mature, it already gives welcome height and definition to this otherwise blank garden.

—— Sundries ——

Soil improver
Pelleted chicken manure or slow-release fertilizer
120 litres cocoa shells or composted bark (or gravel)

—— Tools ——

Hose or watering can
Spade
Tape measure
Pegs or skewers
Rope (washing line or hose will do)
Wheelbarrow or groundsheet

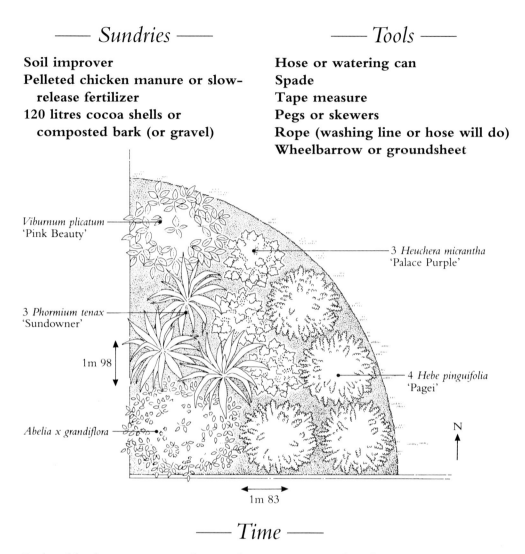

Viburnum plicatum 'Pink Beauty'

3 *Heuchera micrantha* 'Palace Purple'

3 *Phormium tenax* 'Sundowner'

1m 98

4 *Hebe pinguifolia* 'Pagei'

Abelia x grandiflora

N

1m 83

—— Time ——

It should take one person about 3 hours; two people 2 hours.

—— Method ——

1. Give all the plants a thorough watering.

2. Mark out the area of the new bed by measuring along the side of the drive and along the pavement, and putting in pegs or skewers at the relevant points. Lay the rope between them in a gentle outward curve and adjust it till it looks good from all sides. Dig carefully along the inside of the rope to mark the curve permanently, then get rid of the rope and the pegs.

3. Scoop off all the grass by marking out, with the spade, slightly-bigger-than-spade-sized pieces and slicing underneath them, taking as little of the soil with them as possible. Don't waste the grass – put it on the compost heap to rot down. Once you have removed all the grass, dig the soil over and improve it (see page 116). Then level the soil roughly.

4. Set out the plants in their pots on the soil and check the arrangement from all angles to see how it looks.

5. Leaving the other plants in position in their pots, start by planting the central shrub – the phormium(s) in this case – in the usual way (see page 117). Check that it is at the best angle before you fill in the hole with soil. Then plant the rest of the shrubs, moving outwards from the centre, checking each time that the plant is in the right place relative to the others and that it looks good before you fill in the hole.

6. Once all the plants are in, if the soil is dry, give the whole bed a thorough watering and then spread a 5–7 cm (2–3 in) layer of cocoa shells, composted bark or even gravel over the soil to keep the moisture in and the weeds down.

7. As the plants in the front of the bed start to spread out in a year or so, just cut away a little more of the lawn to make room for them.

Single-colour border – shady

~

DESIGNER

Jean Goldberry

There are fashions in gardening as in anything else, and single-colour borders or gardens like the world-famous white garden at Sissinghurst in Kent became very fashionable a few years ago. It's difficult to do it successfully in a large space, but in a small area a single-colour theme can often be the best option, because using lots of colours in a confined space is likely to wind up looking a bit of a mess and giving you a headache! For our first single-colour border – a very small, shady area under the windows of a north-facing house – we opted for white flowers, which really do gleam in shade, and a fair proportion of gold foliage to add brightness and warmth. There are also evergreens to offer something attractive to look at all through the year.

There was quite a lot of wall space – not just the front of the house itself, but a large section of next door's house wall on the east side and the wall of the porch on the west – so climbers were a must.

At its best from early summer, when the clematis starts flowering, to late summer, when the Japanese anemones finish flowering, though with a good skeleton of evergreens it will look good all year.

—— *Plants* ——

5 Japanese anemone (*Anemone ×* *hybrida* **'Honorine Jobert')**
Height/spread: 80 × 40 cm (2½ft × 40 in)

3 Lady fern (*Athyrium filix-femina*)
Height/spread: 1 × 1 m (3 × 3 ft)

1 Mexican orange blossom (*Choisya ternata* 'Sundance')
Height/spread after 10 years: 2 × 2 m (6½ × 6½ ft)

2 *Clematis* 'Miss Bateman'
Height/spread: 2.4 × 2.4 m (8 × 8 ft)

1 Pampas grass (*Cortaderia selloana* 'Goldband')
Height/spread: 1.5 m × 1 m (5 × 3 ft)

3 *Hedera helix* 'Goldheart'
(or 'Buttercup' if you can get it)
Height/spread: 4.5 × 3 m (15 × 10 ft)

3 *Hosta* 'Frances Williams'
Height/spread: 70 × 70 cm (28 × 28 in)

1 Golden hop (*Humulus lupulus* 'Aureus')
Height/spread: 6 × 6 m (20 × 20 ft)

5 *Lysimachia clethroïdes* (or *L. ephemerum*)
Height/spread: 1.2 m × 40 cm (4 ft × 16 in)

5 *Viola cornuta alba*
Height/spread: 12–20 × 20 cm (5–8 × 8 in)

The combination of the golden foliage of the hop and the choisya, with a succession of white flowers from early summer through to autumn, really does bring this shady little bed to life.

Sundries

Soil improver
Pelleted chicken manure or slow-
    release fertilizer
Wire
Masonry nails/washers
120 litres chipped bark

Tools

Hose or watering can
Hammer
Wire snippers
Spade
Trowel

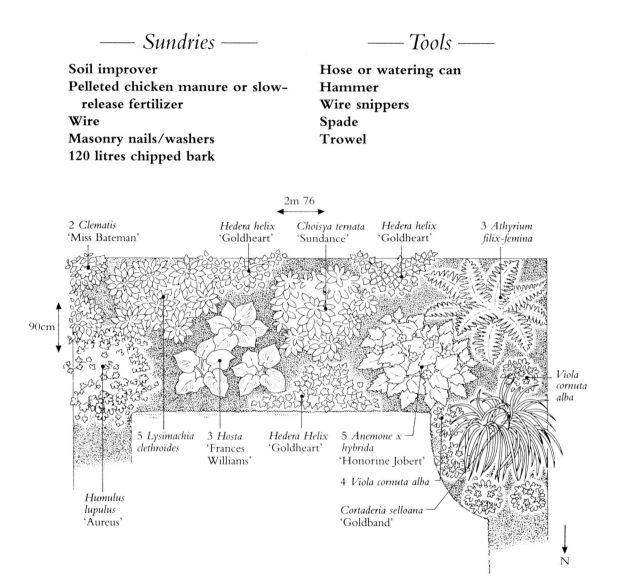

2m 76

2 *Clematis* 'Miss Bateman'

Hedera helix 'Goldheart'

Choisya ternata 'Sundance'

Hedera helix 'Goldheart'

3 *Athyrium filix-femina*

90cm

Viola cornuta alba

5 *Lysimachia clethroïdes*

3 *Hosta* 'Frances Williams'

Hedera Helix 'Goldheart'

5 *Anemone x hybrida* 'Honorine Jobert'

4 *Viola cornuta alba*

Humulus lupulus 'Aureus'

Cortaderia selloana 'Goldband'

N

—— Time ——

It should take two people 2–3 hours; one person 3–4 hours. Wiring the walls is the longest job.

—— Method ——

1. Give all the plants a thorough watering.

2. Put up the wires on the walls (see page 119). It makes sense to do this, which involves treading all over the bed, before you dig.

3. Dig over the bed and improve the soil (see page 116).

4. Set the plants out in their pots and make any necessary adjustments to the way the grouping looks at this stage. Plant in the usual way (see page 117), starting with the climbers and remembering to plant the clematis a good 10–15 cm (4–6 in) deeper than they are in their pots. When all the plants are in, give the bed a thorough watering, then mulch with chipped bark.

5. In late autumn, plant summer snowflakes (*Leucojum aestivum*) for late spring/early summer.

Having cleared the old woody shrubs and climbers from this part of
the border, we chose shrubs and perennials with flowers in a whole
range of blues, many of them with silver or gold variegated foliage.

Single-colour border – sunny

~

DESIGNER

Jean Goldberry

Our second single-colour border gets sun for much of the day as it faces south-east. It is backed by a white wall, which really does show up to perfection any colour growing against it – except white of course! Before we started there was a very woody, straggly honeysuckle on the wall and some elderly neglected roses in the bed in front of it. Since there was masses of honeysuckle elsewhere in the garden and roses in much better condition, we got rid of them all before we started work. To the left of the border were some mature shrubs which we left.

The single colour this time is blue, though the plants we've chosen cover a whole range of blues from pale lavender to deep rich blues and almost-purples. To set it off there is silver and grey foliage, some of it evergreen, with some cream and green as well, and an upright blue-green juniper for structure.

At its best from May to October, though the use of evergreens means that it will look good all year.

—— *Plants* ——

1 Juniper (*Juniperus communis* 'Hibernica')
Height/spread after 10 years: 3–5 m × 30 cm (10–16 × 1 ft)

5 *Agapanthus* Headbourne Hybrids
Height/spread: 80 × 40 cm (2½ ft × 16 in)

1 *Hosta* 'Frances Williams'
Height/spread: 60 × 40 cm (2 ft × 16 in)

3 Lavender (*Lavandula angustifolia* 'Hidcote')
Height/spread after 10 years: 50 × 50 cm (20 × 20 in)

1 *Angelica archangelica*
Height/spread: 2 × 1 m (6½ × 3 ft)

3 Catmint (*Nepeta* 'Six Hills Giant')
Height/spread: 60 × 60 cm (2 × 2 ft)

1 *Miscanthus sinensis* 'Variegatus'
Height/spread: 1.2 m × 45 cm (4 ft × 18 in)

1 large *Yucca gloriosa*
Height/spread after 10 years: 2 × 2 m (6½ × 6½ ft)

3 Rosemary (*Rosmarinus officinalis* 'Miss Jessopp's Upright')
Height/spread after 10 years: 1.8 × 1.8 m (6 × 6 ft)

4 Sea holly (*Eryngium variifolium*)
Height/spread: 45 × 25 cm (18 × 10 in)

5 *Veronica spicata*
Height/spread: 45 × 45 cm (18 × 18 in)

3 *Delphinium grandiflorum* **'Blue Butterfly'**
Height/spread: 45 × 30 cm (18 in × 1 ft)

1 *Clematis* **'Mrs Cholmondeley'**
Height/spread after 10 years: 3.7 × 3.7 m (12 × 12 ft)

1 *Clematis* **'Elsa Späth'**
Height/spread after 10 years: 3.7 × 3.7 m (12 × 12 ft)

1 *Clematis* **'Lasurstern'**
Height/spread after 10 years: 3.7 × 3.7 m (12 × 12 ft)

1 *Clematis × durandii*
Height/spread after 10 years: 2.4 × 2.4 m (8 × 8 ft)

—— *Sundries* ——

Soil improver
Pelleted chicken manure or slow-release fertilizer
Stout wire
Vine eyes: 1 for every 1.2 m (4 ft) of wire
3 **bamboo canes with rubber tip protector(s)**
Garden twine

—— *Tools* ——

Hose or watering can
Hammer
Wire snippers
Spade
Fork

4m 87

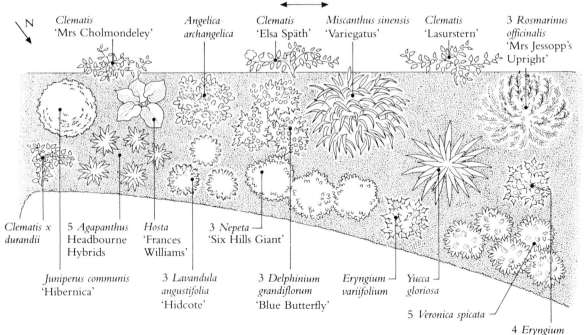

Clematis 'Mrs Cholmondeley'
Angelica archangelica
Clematis 'Elsa Späth'
Miscanthus sinensis 'Variegatus'
Clematis 'Lasurstern'
3 Rosmarinus officinalis 'Mrs Jessopp's Upright'

N

Clematis x durandii
5 Agapanthus Headbourne Hybrids
Hosta 'Frances Williams'
3 Nepeta 'Six Hills Giant'

Juniperus communis 'Hibernica'
3 Lavandula angustifolia 'Hidcote'
3 Delphinium grandiflorum 'Blue Butterfly'
Eryngium variifolium
Yucca gloriosa
5 Veronica spicata
4 Eryngium variifolium

—— *Time* ——

Assuming that the bed is already cleared, it will take two people 2–3 hours; one person 3–4 hours. Putting up the wires is probably the longest job.

—— *Method* ——

1. Give all the plants a thorough soaking.

2. Fix the wires to the walls (see page 119).

3. Dig the bed over, improving the soil (see page 116). Most of these sun-loving plants like very free drainage, so make sure that there is plenty of grit in the soil.

4. Set the plants, still in their pots, out on the soil and ensure that they're in the best possible positions. Remember that some shrubs may be smaller than some herbaceous plants at this stage, but will grow much larger than them eventually, so if it appears that you have something small behind some taller plants, don't panic. If that's what it says on the plan, trust me!

5. Plant in the usual way (see page 117), starting at the wall and working outwards. Remember to plant the clematis 10–15 cm (4–6 in) deeper than they are in their pots. *Clematis × durandii* is unlike most other clematis in that it doesn't cling by its leaf stalks and so needs a bit more support. Make a wigwam with the three 1.2 m (4 ft) bamboo canes, pushing one end of each firmly into the soil and pushing all three top ends, if possible, into one rubber tip protector. That not only holds them all together very easily, but also means that they won't do any damage to eyes should you inadvertently stumble against them. If they're too large to go into one tip protector, tie the ends together with twine and push on a couple of end protectors. Weave the stems of the clematis around the canes and tie them with garden twine. Once they reach the top of the wigwam, tie them all loosely together and they will spill down over the sides.

Herb garden

～

DESIGNER

Maurice Brown

No garden should be without herbs – not only are they invaluable for the kitchen, but they are also first-class garden plants in many instances, with flowers, scent and attractive foliage, often evergreen to boot. You can grow herbs in among other plants, of course, but a small formal herb area can be a very attractive garden feature indeed. Where you site it is important. Most herbs need sun for at least half the day, so find the sunniest spot you can. But you must consider the practicalities too. If you put your herb bed at the bottom of the garden so that picking a sprig of rosemary for the Sunday lamb involves putting on the wellies and a coat in winter, chances are you're not going to bother. A position close to the house with dry access from a path, is the ideal spot, even if it's not quite as sunny as other parts of the garden.

Our garden faced south-east, with sun from early morning till mid-afternoon, and had a narrow flower bed adjoining the patio outside the back door. The soil was very free-draining and rather poor, which suits most herbs, especially those like rosemary, sage and thyme from the Mediterranean. In fact these herbs really won't thrive in wet heavy soils, so if yours is really heavy clay, it might be worth digging out the very small area you'll need – about 1.5×1 m (5×3 ft) – to a spade's depth, dumping the soil, breaking up the bottom of the hole with a fork, then filling it in with some good gritty topsoil.

We planted some of the most popular culinary perennial herbs that are either evergreen, like rosemary and thyme, or will come up every year, like chives and mint, and tarragon, but obviously you can include herbs like parsley and basil which will be killed off by the frost if you like. We also chose some with coloured foliage – fennel and sage, for example – which taste just the same as the plain varieties but look prettier. We've included a mint, the variegated pineapple mint, which is not quite as vigorous as the plain kind but still needs watching. Cut it back when it starts encroaching on its neighbours.

At its best in summer, though there are enough evergreen herbs to make it attractive all year.

The formal pattern of the cobbles makes
the perfect framework for the very informal,
sprawling habit of the herbs.

— Plants —

1 **Rosemary (***Rosmarinus officinalis*** 'Severn Sea')**
Height/spread: 40 × 50 cm (16 × 20 in)

1 **Purple-leaved sage (***Salvia officinalis*** 'Purpurascens')**
Height/spread: 40 × 60 cm (16 in × 2 ft)

1 **Golden thyme (***Thymus ×*** citriodorus*** 'Aureus')**
Height/spread: 10 × 25 cm (4 × 10 in)

1 ***Artemisia dracunculus*** **(French tarragon; it must be French, not the coarser, less aromatic Russian one)**
Height/spread: 45 × 30 cm (18 in × 1 ft)

1 **Marjoram (***Origanum vulgare*** 'Gold Tip')**
Height/spread: 60 × 30 cm (2 × 1 ft)

1 **Rue (***Ruta graveolens*** 'Jackman's Blue')**
Height/spread. 60 × 80 cm (2 × 2½ ft)

1 **Pineapple mint (***Mentha suaveolens*** 'Variegata')**
Height/spread: 75 × 75 cm (29 × 29 in)

1 **Bronze fennel (***Foeniculum vulgare*** 'Purpurea')**
Height/spread: 1.5 m × 60 cm (5 × 2 ft)

1 **Chives divided into two (***Allium schoenoprasum***)**
Height/spread: 25 × 25 cm (10 × 10 in)

— Sundries —

84 **Tegula cobbles (see Stockist list on page 122)**
2 **25 kg sacks ready-mix mortar**

— Tools —

Spade and fork
Tape measure
Wooden pegs
Trowel
Old bucket (or sheet of hardboard)
Spirit level
Hose or watering can

— Time —

It will take two people 3–4 hours; one person 4+ hours over 2 days. Laying out the design will take about 3 hours, but you need to leave the mortar to set for at least 12 (ideally 24) hours before you plant the herbs. Planting will take less than an hour.

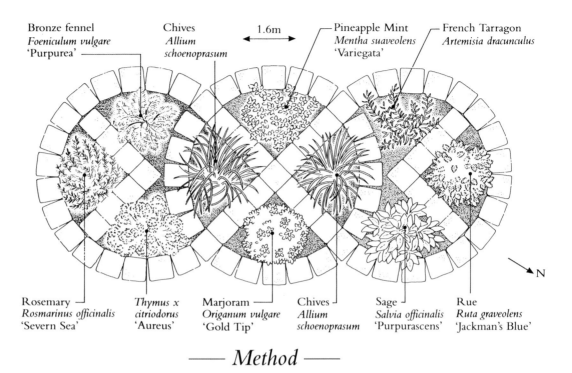

Bronze fennel
Foeniculum vulgare
'Purpurea'

Chives
*Allium
schoenoprasum*

1.6m

Pineapple Mint
Mentha suaveolens
'Variegata'

French Tarragon
Artemisia dracunculus

Rosemary
Rosmarinus officinalis
'Severn Sea'

Thymus x
citriodorus
'Aureus'

Marjoram
Origanum vulgare
'Gold Tip'

Chives
*Allium
schoenoprasum*

Sage
Salvia officinalis
'Purpurascens'

Rue
Ruta graveolens
'Jackman's Blue'

N

— *Method* —

1. Mark out the area and prepare the ground. Once you've dug it, tread it down again as firmly as you can. This may seem perverse, but you want a good firm foundation for the structure, and since you have prepared the soil, loosening it again where necessary to plant the herbs won't be much of a problem.

2. Lay out the cobbles in the pattern on the patio or lawn, close to where you're actually going to build the herb garden, so that you can see what it will look like, and fiddle with it until it's right. Doing this makes it very easy to lay the cobbles on the mortar, taking them one or two at a time and placing them in the corresponding position(s) in the bed itself.

3. You want the finished design to be roughly 5 cm (2 in) above the soil, set on 5 cm (2 in) of mortar, so you need to dig out little trenches 8 cm (3 in) deep, the same depth as each cobble. Mark three wooden pegs with a pencil, 5 cm (2 in) from the top and 8 cm (3 in) below that, then hammer two of them into the soil down to the 5 cm (2 in) mark, one at the top of the centre circle, and the other at the nine o'clock position. Check with a spirit level that they are level and make any adjustments necessary.

4. Measure out and mark the centre point of the design. Hammer in another marked peg, again to the 5 cm (2 in) mark and check with the spirit level and both the other pegs that it's at the right level. Then dig out X-shaped trenches to the lower marks on the pegs.

5. Mix up the mortar in an old bucket. Mix up only a little at a time as it starts to set quite quickly and you don't want to feel pressured into working fast or have to keep chucking out hardening mortar.

6. Take the central stone from the design you've laid out, remove the corresponding peg, put a bit more than 5 cm (2 in) of mortar in the trench, lay the stone on it at 45 degrees to the edge of the patio and tap it gently down. Check with the spirit level, using both remaining pegs, one at a time, that it's at the right height. This central stone is key to getting the design level, so it's worth taking some trouble to get it right.

7. Lay the rest of the X, checking with the spirit level and both pegs after each cobble. Keep standing back and looking at it, to make sure that the lines are straight.

8. To make the circle, dig a curved trench between two arms of the X and lay the blocks as before, checking after each one that the levels are right. You'll find that if you lay each cobble so that the inner corners are just touching those of the neighbouring ones, you'll get a pretty regular circle.

9. Once the central circle is laid, lay the horizontal Vs of the outer part-circles first, then lay the curves in between.

10. Scrape away any excess mortar, but make sure that you leave a generous overlap on each side of the blocks. Although the design won't be taking any weight, you do want the blocks to be held firmly in place.

11. Once the mortar is completely dry, you can plant the herbs, having given them a thorough soaking an hour or two before you're ready to start. Since most herbs prefer poor soil, you don't need to add any fertilizer as you plant. Obviously you can plant the herbs in any of the ten compartments you've created, but it makes for a more attractive arrangement if you balance the design, with tall herbs like rosemary and tarragon at the back and similar low-growing ones at the front.

Mediterranean corner

~

DESIGNER

Jean Goldberry

The sheltered south-facing junction of two white walls that gets sun most of the day was the perfect place for a Mediterranean corner, planted with a range of exotic-looking plants, many of them succulents. It was paved, and since all the planting would be in containers we were able to use some tender plants in the arrangement, which would be taken indoors to a cool greenhouse or unheated porch in the winter. Those that won't survive outside in winter are marked with a T. While we used some terracotta pots, in order to save money and get the height that we needed we also used clay flue liners, straight sections of pipe 23 cm (9 in) in diameter and 18, 30 or 45 cm (7, 12 or 18 in) high, which can be used singly or stacked to give you the variety in height you want. The plants weren't planted directly into the

The shells add an exotic feel to this sunny corner with its mixture of hardy and tender succulents.

flue liners. Instead, we used plastic flowerpots, which fitted snugly into the tops of the liners. One of the plants we chose was an *Agave americana*, which is very handsome but extremely spiky, and so if you have small children it's best avoided or used right at the back of the group where there is absolutely no risk that they might fall on it. Or you could use another plant that looks spiky but has much softer leaves, like a cordyline, a phormium or another yucca.

At its best all summer, when all the plants are in place. There are enough hardy ones for it to look good in winter, too.

—— Plants ——

6 Houseleeks (*Sempervivum*) – any variety with a reddish tinge to the leaves
Height/spread: 10–15 × 20–30 cm (4–6 × 8 in–1 ft)

1 *Aeonium arboreum* 'Zwartkop' T (often sold as 'Schwarzkopf')
Height/spread: 60 cm × 1 m (2 × 3 ft)

6 Clover (*Trifolium repens* 'Wheatfen')
Height/spread: 12 × 30 cm+ (5 in × 1 ft+)

6 *Sedum* 'Ruby Glow'
Height/spread: 10 × 30 cm (4 in × 1 ft)

1 *Agave americana* T
Height/spread: 2 × 2 m (6½ × 6½ ft); smaller in a pot

2 *Yucca filamentosa* 'Variegata'
Height/spread after 10 years: 2 × 2 m (6½ × 6½ ft); smaller in a pot

3 *Echeveria elegans* T
Height/spread: 10 × 50 cm (4 × 20 in)

—— Sundries ——

1 terracotta pot 50 cm (20 in) high
1 terracotta trellis pot 15 cm (6 in) high
1 shallow terracotta dish 7.5 cm (3 in) high
Assorted round clay flue liners 23 cm (9 in) in diameter (see list of stockists, page 122): 2 × 18 cm (7 in) high; 7 × 30 cm (1 ft) high; 1 × 45 cm (18 in) high
7 23 cm (9 in) plastic flowerpots

A few decorative pebbles and/or shells
50 kg (110 lb) soil-based compost with added grit
Broken polystyrene plant trays or packaging for crocking

—— Tools ——

Hose or watering can
Gloves
Knife

—— Time ——

It should take two people about 1 hour; one person about 2 hours.

—— Method ——

1. Give all the plants a thorough watering.

2. Place the flue liners in a line along the two walls and play with the different heights until you get an arrangement you like.

3. Plant up the containers and the plastic flowerpots, using a layer of broken-up polystyrene in the bottom and leaving a good 2.5 cm (1 in) below the rim to allow you to water easily without slopping compost all down the liners.

4. Site the plastic flowerpots in the tops of the flue liners and position the terracotta pots in front of them.

5. Finish off with groups of pebbles and/or shells placed around them.

Remember to take in the tender plants before the first frosts. From late September on, keep an ear open for the weather forecast!

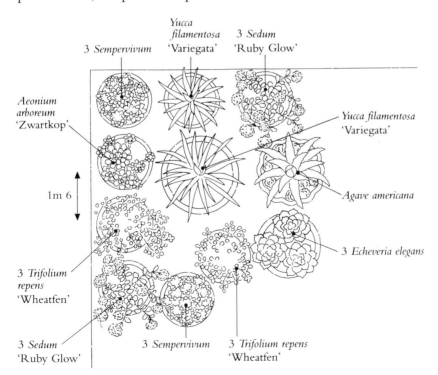

Formal front

~

DESIGNER

Penelope Smith

Lots of terraced Victorian cottages have tiny front gardens – often no more than about 1.8 m (6 ft) deep – and since space is so limited, it can be difficult to choose plants that look good but at the same time don't quickly become too big and cut out much of the light from the sitting-room window. The garden we tackled was 4 m (13 ft) long × 1.8 m (6 ft) deep at its narrowest, facing north-west and so rather shady, laid mainly to gravel with a few old woody hydrangeas growing along the inside of the garden wall.

A formal scheme suggested itself, a tiny parterre – a pattern in clipped box and gravel, with an evergreen feature plant in the centre which would be dramatic but would not grow much taller than when it was planted. That way the garden would look good all through the year. Once the box had reached the desired height, it would be clipped, using a line to keep the top straight – no hardship with such a small amount to do. Once a year would keep it in check and twice a year would have it looking razor sharp.

We settled for an elongated diamond in the centre of the design and a small box triangle at each corner, with a narrow low box hedge running parallel to the path, with an opening in the centre.

At its best in summer when the alchemilla is in flower, but it looks very good all year round.

—— Plants ——

1 standard clipped variegated holly (*Ilex*) or similar trained evergreen
It won't grow much taller, and you just clip the head regularly to keep it small and neat

48 Box (*Buxus sempervirens*) in 2 litre pots
Height/spread after 10 years: 2 × 2 m (6½ × 6½ ft); but trimmed to make a low hedge

8 Lady's Mantle (*Alchemilla mollis*)
Height/spread: 30–45 × 45 cm (1 ft–18 in × 18 in)

—— Sundries ——

Soil improver
Pelleted chicken manure or slow-release fertilizer
25 kg (55 lb) sack gravel
***2* lengths of garden line with a bamboo cane at each end**

—— Tools ——

Hose or watering can
Spade
Trowel
Garden line with a peg at each end
Spare pegs
Tape measure
Secateurs

Although the box is still very small, and not yet ready for clipping, the crisp, geometric pattern is still very clear, adding undoubted style to this tiny gravelled front garden.

—— Time ——

It should take two people 3 hours; one person 4 hours or more.

—— Method ——

1. Give all the plants a thorough watering.

2. Prepare the ground, digging over the area in which you are going to plant, and improve the soil (see page 116). Then level it, treading over it lightly just to compact it a little.

3. Working with the plan and scaling up very carefully, find the top point of the diamond by locating the centre of the bay window or house wall. Work out how far from the wall the first box plant should be, then hammer in a peg. Find the bottom point of the diamond in the same way and mark that too, and then the two points at either side. Given that the diamond has inner and outer dimensions, make sure you always work to the outer ones. Then check by eye that they look right. In this instance *looking* right is more important than being right – fixed points like house walls aren't always 100 per cent true.

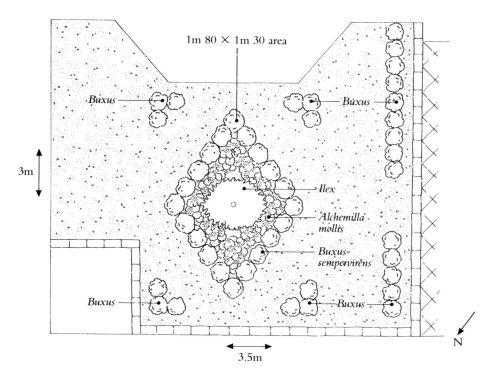

4. Find the central point of the diamond and dig a generous planting hole for the standard holly. Plant in the usual way (see page 117).

5. Replace two adjacent pegs – those at the top and the right of the diamond, for instance – with the pegs on the ends of the line and pull the line taut. Then dig a narrow trench, wide enough to take the root ball of each box plant, along the *inside* of the line. Put in the first two box plants at either end of the trench, one at each point, then plant the rest from alternate ends, working towards the middle. That way you can make any adjustments to the spacing as you go. Plant the box with the stems about 30 cm (1 ft) apart, checking after each one that the line is still straight. It's much easier to adjust one plant than the best part of a row!

6. Plant the other three sides of the diamond in the same way.

7. To plant the triangles, mark out two sides – say, top and right – of the overall area, using a spare peg to mark the right angle in the top right-hand corner. Plant three box to make each triangle.

8. Plant the other three triangles in the same way, standing back after each one to check that it looks right in relation to the others and to the diamond. Then plant up the low hedge running parallel with the path.

9. To encourage bushy growth, just snip off any particularly long shoots. Serious pruning to give the box hedges their razor-sharp lines comes later once the plants have reached the required height.

10. Plant the alchemilla around the holly, and then cover the area with gravel.

11. When you are ready to shape the hedges – when they're a few centimetres taller and wider than you want them to be – set out two lines with bamboo canes at each end, at the desired height and width, and trim carefully to them. It's best done with secateurs, rather than shears or a hedge trimmer, because trimming it shoot by shoot means that the margin for error is much less. It does take longer, but since it's such a tiny area that really is no hardship. Once you are more confident you can trim it with shears.

12. If you make a mistake and snip off too much or the wrong bit, don't panic. The real plus with topiary, as opposed to sculpture, is it will grow back.

Water feature

~

DESIGNER

Penelope Smith

There is no doubt that water is a huge plus in any garden. Acting as a mirror to the sky, it has a calming effect and the sound of running water is very soothing. Many people are rather daunted by the notion of building a pond or think their garden is too small for one. But even the smallest garden has room for this lovely miniature water feature. Water is pumped up from a reservoir, spills out over the rim of a terracotta pot laid on its side and is surrounded by striking foliage plants. The feature is simple to put together and if you use a DIY pump, with an electrical point close by, you don't need an electrician either.

Our garden was a tiny city back yard, only 6 × 5.4 m (20 × 18 ft), facing west. There were some existing evergreen shrubs in the border, but an area near the path where various perennials had got overgrown needed some attention so we decided to site our water feature there. We chose an imitation lead (in fact plastic) patio planter as our water tank because it was as cheap as an overflow tank, and the dark metallic grey colour added a gleam to the water. It's 45 cm (18 in) in diameter, though the slates round the edge make the surface area even smaller, and 35 cm (14 in) deep, and really pretty safe. If you have a toddler and feel a bit uneasy about potential danger, place some stout wire mesh across the top, bend the edges over the rim of the tank and tuck them down into the soil, spreading some small flat pebbles over the surface. You will then get water splashing on to pebbles, which looks very attractive, and then filtering through into the tank.

At its best from spring to late autumn, though attractive all year round.

A very gentle trickle from the rim of the pot barely ruffles the surface of the water into which it falls. The different shapes and textures of the leaves around the pot contrast beautifully with its solid, smooth rounded shape.

—— Plants ——

1 Sacred bamboo (*Nandina domestica* 'Firepower')
Height/spread: 1 m × 60 cm (3 × 2 ft)

1 *Euphorbia wulfenii*
Height/spread: 80 × 80 cm (2½ × 2½ ft)

3 Stinking iris (*Iris foetidissima*)
Height/spread: 60 cm (2 ft) × infinite

3 Ivy (any small, plain green variety will do)
Spread: 1 m (3 ft)

—— Sundries ——

1 tall terracotta pot 35–45 cm (14–18 in) high with a lip and a drainage hole

1 23 litre (5 gallon) plastic tank (a patio planter or overflow tank will do)

1 Mini Cascade pump

2 m (6½ ft) length of 1 cm (½ in) plastic tubing

1 packet Plumberfix

Rubber gloves

Rough pieces of slate – 1 sq m (11 sq ft) will be ample

1 bag 10 cm (4 in) cobbles

—— Tools ——

Hose or watering can
Spade
Fork
Trowel
Spirit level
Hammer

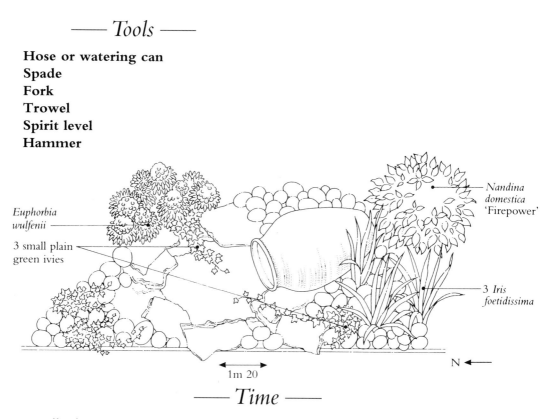

Euphorbia wulfenii

3 small plain green ivies

Nandina domestica 'Firepower'

3 *Iris foetidissima*

1m 20

N ←

—— Time ——

It will take two people about 2–3 hours; one person 3–4 hours.

—— Method ——

1. Attach the plastic tubing to the outflow of the pump, submerse it in a sinkful of water, plug it in and check that it works. You really don't want to finish the job and then find that it doesn't!

2. Decide, approximately, where the pot and tank will go and scratch out the latter's position on the soil. Try out the terracotta pot in various positions until you find the one that looks best – almost certainly at an angle and sloping down to the front. You'll need the lip of the pot to extend about 10 cm (4 in) over the tank, otherwise the water might trickle under the lip and into the soil, not back into the tank. Mark the position of the pot.

3. Remove the terracotta pot and dig a hole large enough to take the tank, leaving it 2.5 cm (1 in) above soil level. This is to stop the soil washing into the water and making it muddy. When the hole is the right depth, put the tank in place and check with a spirit level that it's straight. When it is level, fill in any gaps around the sides with soil to hold it firmly.

4. To get the right flow of water, the bottom of the terracotta pot, where the water will flow in via the drainage hole, needs to be just a little bit higher than the front. Make a shallow depression in the soil to take the front and build up the soil level to raise the back.

5. Put the pump, with the tubing firmly attached, in the bottom of the tank. It doesn't really matter where you put it, though probably the best place is closest to your usual vantage point, because that way you won't see the pump or the tubing. If you can avoid it, don't put it right under the outflow from the terracotta pot because you will almost certainly see it.

6. Bring the tubing up the side of the tank, round the back edge, behind the pot and through the drainage hole in the bottom. You're going to hide the edge of the tank and the tubing with slate and pebbles later, but it makes it easier if you scrape out a shallow groove in the soil around the rim and part-bury the tubing in that.

7. To hold the tubing in place inside the pot and stop any water escaping through the drainage hole, use some Plumberfix to seal the rest of the hole. Do follow the manufacturer's instructions carefully and remember to wear rubber gloves.

8. Take the cable by the shortest sensible route to the power source. Once the plants are in place you can bury it under a bit of soil. It's obviously not wise to bury it first, and then dig because although it's low voltage and won't hurt you, if you do slice through it, you'll have to buy new cable.

9. Lay pieces of slate over the rim of the tank in an informal way, some overlapping.

10. Starting with the larger plants at the back, plant in the usual way (see page 117).

11. Arrange the cobbles over the back edge of the slates and in among the plants.

12. Plug in and switch on.

Island bed – sunny

~

DESIGNER

Thomasina Tarling

Many houses built any time from the 1930s to the present day have very uninspiring front gardens – usually just an expanse of lawn with perhaps a narrow border down the side of the path or drive. These are ideal sites for an island bed, planted with year-round interest and colour in mind. Not only does a bed like this bring the front of the house to life as you and your visitors arrive, but it also gives you something attractive to look at from the living-room windows. You can choose any shape for the bed, though curves – circles or ovals – are probably more attractive than angles.

There's absolutely no reason why you couldn't put an island bed in a back garden too, if you wanted to. Back gardens, however, tend to be used more than front gardens and so it can be difficult to find a suitable spot that doesn't get in the way but at the same times looks right, which almost always means a fairly central position.

Choosing the right position for any island bed is very important and especially in a front garden. It needs to relate in a visually satisfying way to the front of the house, which may mean it's right in the middle of the lawn; or it could relate to some prominent feature like a bay window, which means it may not be central. The best thing to do is mark out the bed, using a piece of rope, on the lawn where you think it might look best, then place the plants still in their pots within it. Walk round it, and view it both from the street and from inside the house. If it doesn't look quite right, try another spot. With our first house – the sunny one – the bed, measuring 1.8 × 1.5 m (6 × 5 ft), was

This island bed is lovely in summer when the roses, lavender and potentilla are in flower, but there are enough evergreens, like the spiky cordyline and the pittosporum, to make sure it looks good in winter too.

lined up with the bay window, which meant that it wasn't central to the garden, but in our shady garden (see page 63) there was hardly any wall between the end of the living-room window and the boundary fence and so we ignored the window and put the bed in the centre of the lawn.

Our sunny garden faced just south of west and so got the sun from just after midday onwards. Apart from some rather patchy grass, it was an entirely plant-free zone. The soil was heavy clay and had therefore to be made free-draining enough for sun-loving plants like lavenders (see page 116).

The plants chosen will provide colour and interest all through the year. Many, like the pittosporum, the cordyline, the hebes and the daphne have evergreen foliage, while the flowering shrubs between them will be in bloom from late winter through to late autumn. The main foliage colour is silver with some plain green and wine red while the flowers are white, pink, blue and purple.

As usual, we planted everything quite close together, with a view to taking some of the plants out in a couple of years and finding them new homes, and, of course, enlarging the bed a little as the plants spread outwards.

At its best from late winter to early autumn, though with a high percentage of evergreens it will look good all year.

—— Plants ——

1 *Pittosporum* '**Garnettii**' or *P. tenuifolium* '**Silver Queen**'
Height/spread after 10 years: 2 × 1 m (6½ × 3 ft)

1 **Cabbage palm (*Cordyline australis*)**
Height/spread after 10 years: 2 × 2 m (6½ × 6½ ft)

1 *Potentilla fruticosa* '**Abbotswood**'
Height/spread after 10 years: 1 × 1 m (3 × 3 ft)

1 *Daphne odora* '**Aureomarginata**'
Height/spread after 10 years: 70 cm × 1 m (28 in × 3 ft)

3 **Rose (*Rosa* 'The Fairy')**
Height/spread after 10 years: 1 × 1 m (3 × 3 ft)

3 *Hebe rakaiensis*
Height/spread after 10 years: 50 cm × 1 m (20 in × 3 ft)

3 **Lavender (*Lavandula angustifolia* 'Hidcote')**
Height/spread after 10 years: 50 × 50 cm (20 × 20 cm)

3 *Artemisia* '**Powis Castle**'
Height/spread: 1 × 1 m (3 × 3 ft)

3 *Euphorbia dulcis* '**Chameleon**'
Height/spread: 30 × 30 cm (1 × 1 ft)

5 **Lily (*Lilium regale*)**
(either as bulbs in spring or as plants in pots in early summer)
Height: 1–2 m (3–6½ ft)

—— Sundries ——

Soil improver
Pelleted chicken manure or slow-
    release fertilizer
Wine bottle filled with dry sand,
    plus a length of string (if
    making a circular bed)
120 litres jumbo bark

—— Tools ——

Hose or watering can
Spade
Fork
Trowel
Garden line with a peg at each
    end (if making an oval bed)
Spare pegs
Tape measure
Wheelbarrow or groundsheet

—— Time ——

It will take two people about 3 hours; one person about 4 hours+.

—— Method ——

1. Give all the plants a thorough watering.

2. Having decided where the bed is going to look best, mark it out. Circles are very easy. Fill an empty wine bottle with dry sand and measure out a length of string to the radius of your circle, plus another 30 cm (1 ft). Tie one end of the string to a peg, push the peg into the ground at the centre point of the bed and tie the other end of the string to the neck of the wine bottle, winding it round and round until the string is exactly the right length and taut. Keeping the string tight, tip the wine bottle up so that the sand starts trickling out and walk round so that the sand describes a perfect circle on the grass. Stick in pegs at regular intervals, because you are bound to disturb some of the sand as you work.

Ovals are slightly more difficult, but not much. Using the garden line, mark out the width of the oval, then with spare pegs mark the top and bottom. At 30 cm (1 ft) intervals, going across the oval from the middle to the left, put in pegs at the top and bottom equidistant from the garden line, the first pair 1.2 m (4 ft) apart – or each one 60 cm (2 ft) from the line – and the second pair 1 m (3 ft) apart – or each one 45 cm (18 in) from the line. Repeat, going from the middle to the right. Loop the garden line round the outside of the pegs, right up against them, fiddle with it until the curve is smooth, then mark out the oval with a spade.

3. Dig out the bed and improve the soil (see page 115).

4. Place the plants on the bed and make any adjustments. Keep walking round it to look at it from all sides: island beds are designed to be seen from all angles and you may find that, while it looks good from the front, you may have obscured the view of something from the back. Island beds need the taller plants in the centre, with a gentle gradation in height down to the edge. Again you may find as you plant that some of the perennials on the outside are bigger than the shrubs in the centre, but don't panic. The shrubs will grow quite quickly to reach their proper size and they will then be bigger than the perennials that surround them.

5. Plant in the usual way (see page 117), starting in the centre with the key shrubs and working your way outwards. The lilies can either be planted as bulbs in the spring or bought in leaf or even in flower in early summer and planted out then.

6. When you've finished planting, give everything a thorough watering and then mulch the bed.

3 *Lavandula angustifolia* 'Hidcote'

1m 96

3 *Euphorbia dulcis* 'Chameleon'

Potentilla fruticosa 'Abbotswood'

Cordyline australis

1m 35

Daphne odora 'Aureomarginata'

3 *Hebe rakaiensis*

3 *Artemesia* 'Powis Castle'

Pittosporum tenuifolium 'Silver Queen'

3 *Rosa* 'The Fairy'

Island bed – shady

~

DESIGNER

Thomasina Tarling

In many ways colour all through the year is even more welcome in a shady north-facing garden like the second one we chose in which to make an island bed. There was already an island bed of sorts – square with a solitary dark green conifer in the centre – but it did nothing to brighten the front of the house.

Gold is always a good colour for a shady spot because it brings its own sunlight with it, and many shrubs with golden or gold-variegated foliage grow very happily in shade. Again the plants are chosen to give colour and interest right through the year, some with their evergreen foliage like the gold-variegated holly, the pale sage-and-cream sisyrinchiums, the hellebores and ferns, and others with a succession of flowers in blue, white and gold from early winter through till autumn.

At its best all year round, with something in flower most of the time.

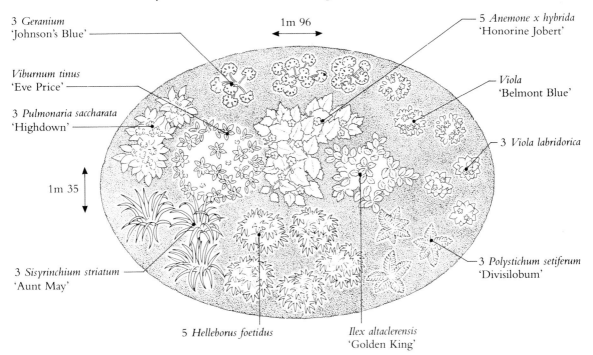

3 *Geranium* 'Johnson's Blue'

1m 96

5 *Anemone x hybrida* 'Honorine Jobert'

Viburnum tinus 'Eve Price'

Viola 'Belmont Blue'

3 *Pulmonaria saccharata* 'Highdown'

3 *Viola labridorica*

1m 35

3 *Polystichum setiferum* 'Divisilobum'

3 *Sisyrinchium striatum* 'Aunt May'

5 *Helleborus foetidus*

Ilex altaclerensis 'Golden King'

—— Plants ——

1 Holly (*Ilex × altaclerensis* 'Golden King')
Height/spread after 10 years: 3 × 2 m (10 × 6 ft)

1 *Viburnum tinus* 'Eve Price'
Height/spread after 10 years: 1.2 × 1.2 m (4 × 4 ft)

5 Hellebore (*Helleborus foetidus*)
Height/spread: 45 × 45 cm (18 × 18 in)

5 Japanese anemone (*Anemone × hybrida* 'Honorine Jobert')
Height/spread: 80 × 40 cm (2½ ft × 16 in)

3 *Geranium* 'Johnson's Blue'
Height/spread: 30 × 60 cm (1 × 2 ft)

3 *Sisyrinchium striatum* 'Aunt May'
Height/spread: 45–60 × 30 cm (18 in–2 ft × 1 ft)

3 Soft shield fern (*Polystichum setiferum* 'Divisilobum')
Height/spread: 60 × 45 cm (2 ft × 18 in)

3 *Viola* 'Belmont Blue'
Height/spread: 12–20 × 20 cm (5–8 × 8 in)

3 *Viola labradorica*
Height/spread: 2.5–5 cm (1–2 in) × infinite

3 Lungwort (*Pulmonaria saccharata* 'Highdown')

—— Sundries ——

Soil improver
Pelleted chicken manure or slow-release fertilizer
Wine bottle filled with dry sand, plus a length of string (if making a circular bed)
120 litres jumbo bark

—— Tools ——

Hose or watering can
Spade
Fork
Trowel
Garden line with a peg at each end (if making an oval bed)
Spare pegs
Tape measure
Wheelbarrow or groundsheet

—— Time ——

It will take two people about 3 hours; one person about 4 hours.

—— Method ——

Mark out the bed, prepare the soil and plant in the same way as for the sunny bed (see page 61).

A striking contrast in foliage shapes and tones ensures that this island bed brightens up this shady garden all year round, with shots of colour from the flowering plants in different seasons.

Brightening up a patio

~

DESIGNER

Jean Goldberry

Many houses, especially relatively new ones, have extremely boring patios which are nothing more than a series of concrete slabs laid in a rectangular grid. Of course, you can do a lot to cheer up such a patio with pots, but you still have to leave a large enough area on which to walk or to put a table and chairs.

One solution would be to rip the whole lot out and start again, but that would obviously cost a lot of money, and for many people the prospect of such major reconstruction is daunting. Yet it is quite astonishing what a difference you can make if you simply relieve the monotony by taking up a couple of slabs here and there and replacing them with a contrasting material. You could use bricks, to match the house, laid in a basket-weave pattern, or if your patio is on a solid base and you don't want to start breaking concrete to give you enough depth for the bricks, you could use paviours the same depth as the old slabs in a similar shade to the bricks.

For our deeply dull patio of weathered cream-coloured slabs we chose to borrow a technique beloved of the Victorians and replace just two slabs with intricate patterns made with pebbles set on edge in cement. We used two different patterns (see below), but if you want to create your own, sketch it out on paper first. It's easier if your design has a central point and is subdivided into smaller areas so that the margin for error is much smaller too.

Between our two pebble patterns we put a shallow bowl planted with evergreen alpines – sempervivums and sedums. They are low enough to keep the eye on the ground where you want it to be, and decorative enough to fit in very well with the patterns.

At its best all year round.

What a difference these two panels of pebbles make to this otherwise very dull patio. And what better way to display pebbles you may have brought back from your holidays.

—— Plants ——

2 *Sedums*
3 **Houseleeks (*Sempervivum*)**
 Height/spread: 10–15 × 20–30 cm (4–6 in × 8 in–1 ft)

***Ophiopogon planiscapus* 'Nigrescens'**

—— Tools ——

Hose or watering can
Spade
Builder's trowel
Soft brush (for rubbing in)

—— Sundries ——

1 shallow bowl 30–40 cm (12–16 in) in diameter

Piece of card a quarter the size of a slab
Sheet of hardboard or heavy-duty plastic (for mixing the ready-mix)
Thick piece of wood about twice the width of a slab
25 litres compost suitable for alpines
Plastic flowerpots
Plastic sack (optional)
Cement remover (optional)

PER SLAB
0.25 kg bag ready-mix sand and cement
1 **squirt washing-up liquid**
1 **bag Cempack 40 mm Arran Pebbles**

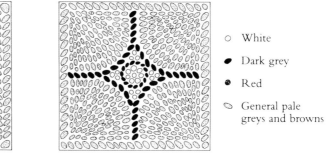

○ White
● Dark grey
◉ Red
▽ General pale greys and browns

—— Time ——

This is really a one-person job, although someone else can help a bit by sorting out the pebbles into different shades; it will take one person 1½–2 hours per slab.

—— Method ——

1. Remove the slabs you intend replacing with pebbles.

2. Sort out the pebbles into broadly similar colours and put the numbers of each you'll need into empty plastic flowerpots.

3. Mix up the ready-mix cement with the trowel, adding just a little water at a time to make a good stiff consistency. You could mix it up in the space you're working on if you're a careful worker, or on the piece of hardboard or plastic. Add a good squirt of washing-up liquid to the finished mix and work it well in. This makes it very smooth and easy to work.

4. Level the mixture within the space so that it's about 1 cm (½ in) below the level of the surrounding slabs and smooth the surface with the trowel.

5. Locate the position of the central pebble by holding the piece of card in the top right-hand corner of the space, just above the cement. The lower left-hand corner of the card gives you the centre point. This may seem a bit fiddly, but if you don't get the central pebble right, it will throw the whole design.

6. Push the pebble, on edge, into the cement so that it's just a bit more than half-buried. Carry on laying the pebbles on edge, working on one area at a time. Every now and then place the piece of wood widthways across the design and, with your hands on either end, press gently down until the wood is touching the slabs on either side. Do the same with the wood lengthways. This ensures that the pebbles are all at the same level.

7. If you want to stop and have a break, cover the area with a plastic sack to prevent the cement from drying out.

8. When all the pebbles are in and have been levelled, take the soft brush and, following the direction of the pattern, brush the cement up and around the pebbles. This ensures that they are held firmly in the cement with no gaps at the sides. Rinse the brush when you've finished and leave to dry.

9. Four or five hours later, when the cement is virtually set, take the soft brush and a bowl of water and, with the dampened bristles, brush the dried cement off the top of the pebbles. Alternatively leave it to set until the following day, then brush the pebbles with cement remover. Do make sure that you rinse them well with plenty of clean water when you've finished, otherwise the chemical will go on working.

10. Plant up the shallow bowl using a compost suitable for alpines and place it on the patio.

Disguising a fence

~

DESIGNER

Judith Sharpe

Many modern gardens are broader than they're long, which means that the boundary at the bottom of the garden, particularly if it's a hard structure like a wall or a fence, can seem very dominant. One way of making it appear to recede is by planting pale smoky colours in front of it because, while bright colours foreshorten, pastel shades seem further away.

We planted up a half-moon-shaped bed in front of a fence which faced west. The soil was rather sandy and free-draining, and the plants we chose all enjoyed these conditions. The colour scheme, mainly silver and smoky purple foliage with soft pink and white flowers, was designed to push the fence back – visually at least.

At its best from May to September when everything is in flower, though there is some interest all year.

—— *Plants* ——

3 Canary Island ivy (*Hedera canariensis* 'Gloire de Marengo')
Height/spread after 10 years: 3.7 × 3.7 m (12 × 12 ft)

1 Weeping silver-leaved pear (*Pyrus salicifolia* 'Pendula')
Height/spread after 10 years: 5 × 4 m (16 × 13 ft)

1 Smoke bush (*Cotinus coggygria* 'Royal Purple')
Height/spread after 10 years: 3 × 3 m (10 × 10 ft); ideally prune every year or two to get the best-coloured leaves

1 *Lavatera assurgentiflora* 'Barnsley'
Height/spread after 10 years: 3 × 3 m (10 × 10 ft); best cut back very hard each spring

1 Rose (*Rosa* 'Felicia')
Height/spread after 10 years: 1.5 × 2 m (5 × 6½ ft)

1 large or 3 small *Phormium tenax* 'Purpureum'
Height/spread after 10 years: 1.5 × 2 m (5 × 6½ ft)

3 *Salvia officinalis* 'Purpurascens'
Height/spread after 10 years: 40 × 60 cm (16 in × 2 ft)

3 Lavender (*Lavandula angustifolia* 'Rosea')
Height/spread after 10 years: 80 × 80 cm (2½ × 2½ ft)

3 Lambs' lugs (*Stachys olympica*)
Height/spread after 10 years: 25 × 40 cm (10 × 16 in)

The combination of pale flower colours and smoky foliages works very well to disguise the fence and make it appear to recede.

Sundries

Soil improver

Pelleted chicken manure or slow-release fertilizer

120 litres jumbo bark or cocoa shells

Tools

Hose or watering can

Spade

Fork

Tape measure

Rope (washing line or hose will do) *or* measuring line (a length of string with a wooden peg at each end will do) and 8–10 pegs or skewers

Wheelbarrow or groundsheet

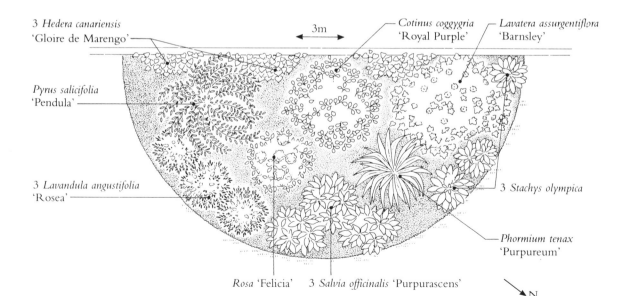

3 *Hedera canariensis* 'Gloire de Marengo'

Pyrus salicifolia 'Pendula'

3 *Lavandula angustifolia* 'Rosea'

3m

Cotinus coggygria 'Royal Purple'

Lavatera assurgentiflora 'Barnsley'

3 *Stachys olympica*

Phormium tenax 'Purpureum'

Rosa 'Felicia'   3 *Salvia officinalis* 'Purpurascens'

N

—— *Time* ——

It will take two people 3 hours, one person 4 hours.

—— *Method* ——

1. Give all the plants a thorough watering.

2. Mark out the bed. If you have a good eye, measure the diameter of the half-moon bed along the back of the fence and then make the curve free-hand on the grass with rope. If you don't have a good eye, measure the diameter along the fence and mark it at each end. Then find the centre point and stick one peg (A) attached to the measuring line firmly into the soil. Unwind the line until the other peg (B) lines up with one of the diameter marks, which will give you the radius. Swing peg B in a semi-circle, stopping at regular intervals and pushing in pegs or skewers to mark the spot. When you've finished, you'll have a perfect semi-circle of markers.

3. Push the spade a few centimetres into the soil all around the curve to mark it permanently, then pull out the markers. Remove the grass, taking as little soil with it as possible, and dig the bed over. (Alternatively, if you can be patient, you can kill off the grass with a glyphosate-based weedkiller, but it would mean waiting 10–14 days for it to die in spring or summer – longer in winter – and then digging the dead grass in.) Do what needs to be done to make your soil free-draining and fertile (see page 116).

4. Lay out the plants in their pots and check that the grouping looks good – primarily from the angle from which you'll see it most often.

5. Plant in the usual way (see page 117), starting with the ivies on the fence. They are self-clinging and thus don't need support once they are producing new growth, so plant them accordingly (see page 119). Work back from the fence, checking as you go that each plant is in the right place before you fill in the planting hole.

6. When all the plants are in, spread a 5–7.5 cm (2–3 in) layer of jumbo bark or cocoa shells over the soil to keep moisture in and weeds down.

Sitting pretty

~

DESIGNER

Penelope Smith

Everyone with a garden needs somewhere to sit back and enjoy it, and there's no reason not to make an attractive feature out of it into the bargain, and of course to increase the pleasure by surrounding it with lots of scented plants.

The garden we chose already had a seat – simply a chain-store bench – in a sunny spot facing south-east, but it was set against a blank red-brick wall belonging to the house next door, with just a couple of bare wooden plant boxes on either side, and really didn't look very inviting at all.

First of all, we decided to put an easy-to-assemble off-the-peg rose arch – an attractive new addition to the Agriframes range with lattice infills up the sides – over it to give it impact. It's a free-standing one, with legs that are just pushed into the soil (the kit comes with a special hole-making tool, so it really is very easy to do), and therefore doesn't need to be attached to the wall. It would be very useful to be able to fix some wires or even just a few lead-headed nails to the wall (see page 119), though, to support the wall shrubs, but if the wall belongs to the neighbours do ask their permission first.

To grow over and around it we chose a range of plants to give colour – mainly yellows and whites, with just a touch of blue – and in most cases scent for the longest possible season. So there's the small new *Choisya* 'Aztec Pearl' with scented flowers in spring/early summer (and often again in late summer), followed by the pineapple broom (*Cytisus battandieri*) which has plumes of egg-yolk yellow, pineapple-scented flowers, a yellow climbing rose and a very fragrant honeysuckle over the arch, with lavender and thyme planted around the seat. Thyme releases its scent when it's crushed, and can withstand being trodden on now and then. A number of the plants are evergreen, so the area will look good all year round. As a finishing touch there's a terracotta mini-Ali Baba pot planted with a lovely, trailing, blue-green euphorbia.

These sun-loving plants all need a free-draining soil.

At its best from late spring to autumn when all the shrubs and climbers flower, though the evergreens will ensure that it looks good all year.

Once the honeysuckle and the rose have reached the top of the arch, they will form a wonderfully fragrant bower, while the wall plants on either side will spread to cover more and more of the rather bleak brick.

75

—— Plants ——

1 Pineapple broom (*Cytisus battandieri*)
Height/spread after 10 years: 5 × 5 m (16 × 16 ft)

1 *Ceanothus* 'Yankee Point'
Height/spread after 10 years: 3 × 3 m (10 × 10 ft)

***Choisya* 'Aztec Pearl'**
Height/spread after 10 years: 2.4 × 2.4 m (8 × 8 ft)

1 Rose (*Rosa* 'Golden Showers')
Height after 10 years: 3 m (10 ft)

1 Honeysuckle (*Lonicera japonica* 'Halliana')
Height/spread after 10 years: 5 × 5 m (16 × 16 ft)

1 Lavender (*Lavandula angustifolia* 'Munstead')
Height/spread after 10 years: 45 × 45 cm (18 × 18 in)

2 Thyme (*Thymus vulgaris* 'Silver Posie')
Height/spread after 10 years: 15 × 30 cm (6 in × 1 ft)

1 *Euphorbia myrsinites*
Height/spread: 8 × 25 cm (3 × 10 in)

—— Sundries ——

Soil improver
Pelleted chicken manure or slow-release fertilizer
1 1.8 m (6 ft) rose arch with lattice infills
1 terracotta pot around 45–60 cm (18 in–2 ft) tall
1 plastic flowerpot (to fit in the top of the terracotta pot)
5 litres gritty potting compost
Lead-headed nails (for the wall plants)
Soft garden twine

—— Tools ——

Hose or watering can
Spade
Fork
Wire cutters
Hammer

—— Time ——

It will take two people about 3 hours; one person about 4–5 hours.

—— Method ——

1. Give all the plants a thorough watering.

2. Dig over the area for planting and improve the soil (see page 116).

3. Wire the wall (see page 119).

4. Assemble the arch, according to the instructions, and put it in position, using the special hole-making tool provided to make the holes for the legs.

5. Plant the ceanothus and the *Cytisus battandieri*, one on each side of the arch, by the wall. Take care not to plant them too close to it, though, because the soil there will be very dry indeed. Hammer a few lead-headed nails into the mortar between the bricks on the wall and attach the branches to them. Prune off any growths that are directly forward-facing.

6. Plant the climbing rose and the honeysuckle, weaving the stems in and out of the arch's latticework if they are flexible enough, or tying them in if they're not.

7. Plant the remaining shrubs and herbs near and even under the seat.

8. Plant the euphorbia in gritty compost in the plastic flowerpot and sit it inside the terracotta pot. Filling the whole terracotta pot with compost would make it very heavy and is quite unnecessary since the plant doesn't need a vast depth of compost in which to thrive.

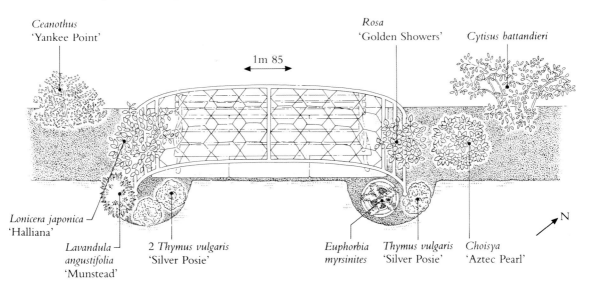

A pleasure to walk along! As the plants begin to spread, their roots will stabilize the slabs and their foliage will soften the hard materials still more.

Alpine path

~

DESIGNER

Maurice Brown

Most of us need a path in the garden for purely practical reasons – getting from A to B without getting wet and muddy feet in winter, for example – but in too many gardens, paths are purely utilitarian. It seems such a shame when they could be really decorative and, in very small gardens, another welcome opportunity to grow plants. A very simple way is to make an alpine path, with slabs laid on the soil, surrounded by gravel, into which you can plant a whole range of colourful alpines. There is no mortar or cement involved here, although you will need to put wooden shuttering in place on either side of the path to contain the gravel and stop it spreading all over the garden. Incidentally you *must* use Tannalized timber, which is pressure-treated to prevent rotting, and since the wood is going to be surrounded by damp soil, anything else would rot quite quickly.

In our garden the wooden shuttering was already in place, to contain an existing informal path of coarse bark leading down from the lawn, between a raised bed on one side and a wild area on the other, to the bottom of the garden. In this instance, to hold back the soil on either side but at the same time to keep the level of the path the same as that of the lawn from which you step on to it, the shuttering was slightly higher than the path. If you're creating a path from scratch in lawn or bare soil, you can make the shuttering the same height as the path, or just a fraction higher to stop the gravel spilling out.

The garden was south-facing, although a number of large trees in neighbouring gardens meant that there was some dappled shade. The soil was already reasonably free-draining, but since alpines need very free-draining, gritty soil we added some gravel to it as we dug it over.

There are hundreds of lovely alpines to choose from, so it's worth getting a wide range not just of flower colours, but of flowering times too – you should be able to have something in flower from early spring right the way through to late autumn – not forgetting the benefits of foliage colour. There are glorious wine reds, silvers, blues, greys and bright golds as well as lots of different greens, and of course by choosing at least some evergreens (marked with an E in the list below) you can make sure that your alpine path is pretty all through the year. You should allow at least one plant for each slab, with a few extras. A few spring-flowering bulbs, like anemones or small tulips, will add early spring colour, and die away by mid-summer.

At its best from early spring to late summer when the plants will flower in succession, but since most of them are evergreen it will look good all year.

—— Plants ——

1 *Saxifraga* **'Apple Blossom'**
Height/spread: 5 cm (2 in) × infinite

1 *Saxifraga* **'Silver Cushion'**
Height/spread: 15 × 35 cm (6 × 14 in)

1 *Arenaria caespitosa* **'Aurea'** E
Height/spread: 5 × 3- cm (2 in × 1 ft)

1 *Armeria maritima* **'Dusseldorf Pride'** E
Height/spread: 15–20 × 10 cm (6–8 × 4 in)

Edelweiss (*Leontopodium alpinum***)**
Height/spread: 15–20 × 15–20 cm (6–8 × 6–8 in)

1 *Sedum spathulifolium* **'Cape Blanco'** E
Height/spread: 8 × 40 cm (3 × 16 in)

1 *Ajuga reptans* **'Braunherz'** E
Height/spread: 15 × 45 cm (6 × 18 in)

1 **Gentian (***Gentiana* **'Strathmore')**
(needs an *acid* soil)
Height/spread: 5 × 10 cm (2 × 4 in)

1 *Geranium* × *cantabrigiense* **'Biokovo'** semi-E
Height/spread: 15–20 × 30 cm (6–8 in × 1 ft)

1 **Thyme (***Thymus camphoratus***)** E
Height/spread: 1 × 30 cm (½ in × 1 ft)

1 *Campanula garganica* **'Dickson's Gold'**
Height/spread: 5 × 30 cm (2 in × 1 ft)

1 *Sedum* **'Ruby Glow'** E
Height/spread: 5 × 30 cm (2 in × 1 ft)

—— Sundries ——

FOR EACH 4 M (13 FT) OF PATH

4 **Tannalized planks 2 m × 7.5 cm × 2.5 cm (6½ ft × 3 in × 1 in)**

24 **Tannalized pegs 30 × 2.5 × 2.5 cm (1 ft × 1 in × 1 in)**

50 **25 mm (1 in) galvanized nails**

10 **Heritage slabs 45 × 45 cm (18 × 18 in)**

2 **50 kg (110 lb) bags pea gravel**

1 **70 litre bag composted bark or coir**

—— Tools ——

Tape measure
2 garden lines
Spirit level
Hammer
Spade
Fork
Rake
Trowel
Hose or watering can

—— Time ——

It will take two people about 4–5 hours; one person 5–6 hours.

—— Method ——

1. Give all the plants a thorough watering.

2. Measure out the dimension of your path, 7.5 cm (3 in) wider than the slabs on each side, using the garden line and then mark the position with pegs.

3. Dig out the soil to a depth of 7.5 cm (3 in) – the width of a plank – then hammer the pegs, marked at 7.5 cm (3 in) from the top, into the soil *outside* where the shuttering will be. The pegs should be 40 cm (16 in) apart, their tops level with the soil.

4. Put the first plank in position and nail through it into the first peg. Don't hammer it fully home yet, though. Hold the other end of the plank level with the top of the last peg and check with a spirit level that it's straight. If it's not, hammer down whichever of the two pegs is too high (the one at the opposite end to the bubble in the spirit level). When the plank is perfectly level, nail it to the last peg, and then nail it to all the intervening pegs.

5. Fix the plank on the other side in the same way, checking with the spirit level that it's at the same height as the one opposite as well as checking that it's level.

6. When all the shuttering is in place, mix some of the soil you've dug out with equal parts by volume (bucketfuls, in other words) of gravel or coarse grit and some fine organic matter like composted bark or coir. If the soil is already very gritty, add only about half the amount of gravel or grit.

7. Spread the mixture over the path, levelling it roughly with the rake. It should come almost to the top of the shuttering. Then tread it down firmly, putting your weight on your heels and taking very small steps, so that you cover every bit of ground. This part is very important, because if the ground isn't very firm the slabs will sink. (One or two may sink slightly anyway, but it's no big deal to lift the odd slab and put a bit more soil underneath it. However, you'll find that as the plants get established

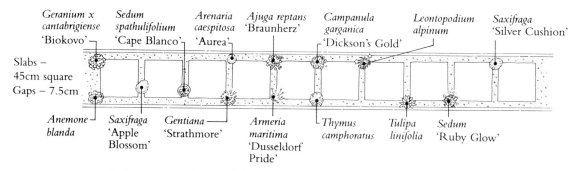

Geranium x cantabrigiense 'Biokovo'   Sedum spathulifolium 'Cape Blanco'   Arenaria caespitosa 'Aurea'   Ajuga reptans 'Braunherz'   Campanula garganica 'Dickson's Gold'   Leontopodium alpinum   Saxifraga 'Silver Cushion'

Slabs – 45cm square Gaps – 7.5cm

Anemone blanda   Saxifraga 'Apple Blossom'   Gentiana 'Strathmore'   Armeria maritima 'Dusseldorf Pride'   Thymus camphoratus   Tulipa linifolia   Sedum 'Ruby Glow'

their roots will soon bind the soil together and stabilize the slabs.) When you've firmed it all, just rake the top level. The soil should now be a couple of centimetres or so (just under 1 in) below the top of the shuttering.

8. To make sure that you lay the slabs in the middle of the path, either set up two lines 7.5 cm (3 in) in from the shuttering or find a piece of wood 7.5 cm (3 in) thick and use it to check that the gap on each side is right.

9. Put the first slab in position and then tap it down, using the wooden handle of a hammer, until it is level with the top of the shuttering. Since the surface of many slabs isn't even because it has a riven effect, a spirit level won't necessarily give you an accurate reading. A straight edge – a plank or even the edge of the spirit level if it's long enough – and a critical eye is probably the best bet.

10. You can lay the next slab 7.5 cm (3 in) from the first or you can make the gap wider if you prefer. We actually made the gaps between twice as wide – 15 cm (6 in) – because it gave us more growing space for the plants, but still allowed us to step comfortably from slab to slab.

11. Once all the slabs are down, spread the pea gravel between them to just below the top of the shuttering.

12. Then plant the alpines in the gaps. Put them wherever you like, but corners and edges are probably more practical than bang in the middle of the space between slabs because, although they will spread over the slabs, it's better to leave the central area free for walking on. You could plant the alpines before you spread the gravel, but doing it this way ensures that each plant gets a bit more gravel in its planting hole.

13. Water thoroughly.

Pots for winter

～

DESIGNER

Penelope Smith

Everyone knows the value of summer bedding for bringing colour to any garden, especially in difficult areas where containers are the only option. And yet many gardeners haven't yet cottoned on to the fact that there are winter bedding plants which will give you colour at a time of year when, if anything, you appreciate it even more. Admittedly the range of plants available for winter isn't as large, but even so there are enough around to make very attractive combinations.

The key plants in our three containers are cabbages. That's right – cabbages, the ornamental ones with wonderfully colourful cream, pink and purple foliage, some with smooth leaves, some with very jagged ones. And we have built the colour scheme around them, using winter-flowering pansies and hardy cyclamen. Using just one type of plant in a large pot can look stunning.

At its best September to January.

—— Plants ——

6 ornamental cabbages
 (5 with smooth leaves, 1 with jagged leaves)
12 pink winter-flowering pansies
8 white winter-flowering pansies
3 hardy cyclamen

—— Tools ——

Hose or watering can
Garden knife
Trowel

—— Sundries ——

3 **terracotta pots: 50 cm (20 in), 38 cm (15 in) and 25 cm (10 in)**
1 **25 litre bag general-purpose compost**
3 **broken polystyrene plant trays or packaging (for crocking)**

—— Time ——

It should take one person about an hour.

—— Method ——

1. Give all the plants a thorough watering.

2. Break up the polystyrene plant trays and put a good deep layer in the bottom of each pot. Since you are growing only annuals which will be replaced in the spring, you don't need a great depth of compost.

3. Plant the jagged cabbage in the centre of the largest pot and four smooth-leaved ones around it.

4. Place the remaining cabbage in the centre of the middle pot and fill it up with the pink pansies.

5. Fill the remaining pot with white pansies and hardy cyclamen.

6. Give all the pots a thorough soaking.

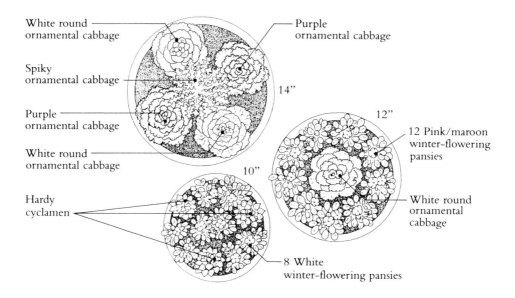

White round ornamental cabbage

Spiky ornamental cabbage

Purple ornamental cabbage

White round ornamental cabbage

Hardy cyclamen

Purple ornamental cabbage

14"

12"

12 Pink/maroon winter-flowering pansies

White round ornamental cabbage

10"

8 White winter-flowering pansies

The rich pinky-maroon of the ornamental cabbages dictates the colours of the pansies and cyclamen planted with them to liven up a patio in winter.

This little formal vegetable garden will be constantly changing from season to season as the crops are harvested and new ones planted.

Mini vegetable plot

~

DESIGNER

Jean Goldberry

Lots of new gardeners with very small gardens are wary of growing vegetables. They think either that you must have imbibed the wisdom at your father's (or, even better, your grandfather's) knee from the time you could toddle, or that you must have masses of space, or that vegetable plots are ugly and best hidden away in a corner, something that's just not practical in a very small garden. This mini-vegetable garden sets out to prove them wrong on all three counts: it's very small; it will look very pretty with its timber edgings, small feature fruit trees and pots of salad crops; and, because you aren't setting out to feed a family of ten all year round, you can afford to buy the few plants you need in the relevant seasons from the garden centre if the idea of sowing even the easiest-to-grow of seeds, like spring onions, makes you nervous – at least in the first season. Once you've tasted vegetables picked only minutes before you eat them, you will be hooked!

By using Tannalized timber boards to contain the beds, we are raising the level of the soil, with plenty of organic matter dug into it, creating a good depth of rich fertile soil which allows us to grow the crops much closer together than we otherwise could. If you have a heavy clay soil, raising the beds also helps improve drainage. Putting a gravelled area in the centre of the layout gives you access to all parts of the bed without ever having to tread on the soil.

The plot we chose faced south, under the kitchen window, bounded on one side by the patio and on the other by the end of the house. We chose to work within those dimensions.

If you're nervous of using a saw, get your local timber merchant to cut the planks to length for you. Bear in mind, when you're working out the sizes of timber you need for your patch, that you must allow for the *width* of the planks. Otherwise you could find you're several centimetres out, and if you are working in a confined space and can't simply make the whole area that bit bigger, that is a real blow.

When it comes to choosing vegetables, the important thing to bear in mind first and foremost is what you like to eat. There's no point in growing spinach if no one in the house likes it. Second, think about the best use of space. A single courgette plant, for example, would fill up about a quarter of the whole plot, and when it would be cropping, courgettes are plentiful and very cheap in the shops. Grow a few new potatoes just for the sheer bliss of eating them 20 minutes after they've come out of the ground, but don't waste your time on maincrop. Salad crops are well worth including both summer and winter, because they taste completely different when they're fresh from the way they do when they've been sitting in a polythene bag for a week, especially if you choose 'pick and come again' salad-bowl varieties where you take only the leaves you need and the plant stays in the ground to produce more. In our pots we grew salad herbs like rocket, which gives a wonderful bite to a green salad and a few leaves of which cost a fortune in the supermarket.

To give our mini-veg. plot structure and height we cheated a little by including fruit. There are two different varieties of Ballerina apples, which make very narrow columns and don't grow very tall, and which will pollinate each other. There is also a standard fig. Trained standard fruit bushes – gooseberries, redcurrants, as well as figs – are excellent for a very small plot because they allow you to grow other crops underneath them. They are becoming much more widely available in garden centres now, and of course you can always order one.

We planted our mini-vegetable garden in early August, so the emphasis was on autumn and winter crops. If you plant in the spring, choose varieties that will crop in summer.

At its best in spring and summer, but attractive and productive in winter too.

—— *Plants* ——

2 Ballerina apples

(ideally different varieties that will pollinate each other: 'Charlotte' is a cooker, 'Waltz' and 'Flamenco' among the best of the eaters)

Height/spread after 10 years: 3 m × 30–40 cm (10 ft × 12–16 in)

1 standard fig

(the fact that its roots are restricted in a pot means it won't grow much larger than it is now)

8 climbing French beans 'Blue Lake'

12 small lettuce 'Salad Bowl'

12 broccoli 'Early Purple Sprouting'

1 tray leeks 'King Richard' or 1lb shallots

6 ruby or rhubarb chard

SEED
Spinach 'Norvak'
Perpetual spinach beet
Spring onion 'White Lisbon
  Winter Hardy'

Carrot 'Autumn King' or
  'Chantenay Red Cored'
Land or American cress
Rocket
Salad burnet

—— Sundries ——

12 sharpened stakes 30 × 2.5 ×
  2.5 cm (1 ft × 1 in × 1 in)
50 2.5 cm (1 in) galvanized nails
1 70 litre bag compost
2 sq m (21½ sq ft) weed-control
  membrane (or black polythene)
1 50 kg sack gravel
2 terracotta pots
8 bamboo canes
Garden twine

TANNALIZED BOARDS
2 1.8 m × 10 cm × 2.5 cm (6 ft ×
  4 in × 1 in)
2 60 × 10 × 2.5 cm (2 ft × 4 in ×
  1 in)
5 50 × 10 × 2.5 cm (20 × 4 × 1 in)
2 70 × 10 × 2.5 cm (28 × 4 × 1 n)
1 1.4 m × 10 cm × 2.5 cm (4½ft ×
  4 in × 1 in)

—— Tools ——

Tape measure
Garden line
Pegs
Spirit level
Spade
Fork

Trowel
Dibber (a pencil will do)
Hammer
Scissors
Long metal spike (optional but
  useful)

—— Time ——

It will take two people 5–6 hours, and it really is much easier with two pairs of hands, but you can manage on your own, though it will take you 7–8 hours.

—— Method ——

1. Measure and mark out the design, then dig over the areas which are to be planted, adding compost as you go. Pile the soil away from the edges a bit, to allow you to fix the planks easily.

2. Mark the pegs at 7.5 cm (3 in), the height above the soil level at which you want them to finish, and at 10 cm (4 in), the depth of the boards. The finished framework will be 2.5 cm (1 in) below soil level, 7.5 cm (3 in) above it.

3. Put in the first peg at the end of one long side, bearing in mind that the pegs go on the inside of the boards wherever possible, though on some corners in the middle of the design geometry dictates that they go outside. It's helpful to make a hole with a long metal spike before you hammer in the peg, because then you'll know that the peg isn't going to hit a stone half-way down and twist out of alignment. Make sure that the 7.5 cm (3 in) mark on the peg is level with the soil *outside* the bed.

4. Nail the first of the two longest boards to the peg, but don't hammer it home. Hammer in another peg at the end of that first long side, hold the board level with the top and check with a spirit level that it's straight. If it's not, tap down the higher of the two pegs. When it's level, nail the board to the second peg and hammer home the first nail.

5. Working towards the middle, fix the next few boards in the same way, checking at each stage with the spirit level, but stop when you're ready to fix the central board. Then work from the other side towards the middle, and fix the central board last. Doing it this way means that if your calculations were just a bit out, you can easily make any necessary adjustments to the length of the central board.

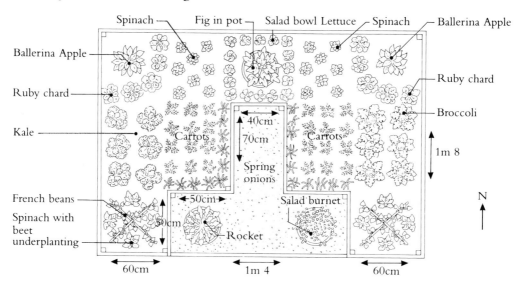

6. Make a very narrow trench with a spade, about 75 cm (3 in) deep, at the front of the bed where it joins the lawn and put in the final board. It needs to be just proud of the surface to keep the gravel in, but not too proud that you trip over it every time you step on to the gravelled area. Hammer the board down to make it a good tight fit and check it with the spirit level. When it's level, pack soil into any gaps at the back and hammer the soil down. It sounds odd, but it really will make sure the board is firmly held.

7. Once the edging is in, level the soil in the bed, and if you need to raise the level a bit more, dig in more compost.

8. Now for the planting. Start with the fig, still in its pot, just leaving the rim above soil level. If you planted it in the usual way, it would grow much too big. Containing the roots like this will keep it small and encourage it to produce fruit, not branches and foliage. Plant the two Ballerina apples. (See page 117 for planting instructions.)

9. Make two wigwams, each out of the four bamboo canes, in the two corners at the front and train the climbing French beans up them. Sow spinach beet seed underneath to make maximum use of the space. By the time the beans have finished producing and are ready to be taken out, the spinach beet, which is happy in partial shade, will be growing nicely.

10. The aim is to make the bed as decorative as possible, so plant the lettuces about 12 cm (5 in) apart in a square around the fig, the ruby chard in a semi-circle around the apple trees, the purple sprouting broccoli in blocks and the spring onions, leeks or shallots in an L-shape following the line of the boards.

11. Sow the rest of the seed (the carrots and spinach) in blocks.

12. Sow the two terracotta pots with rocket and salad burnet or land cress (very like watercress in flavour, but much easier to grow) or use plants if you can find them.

13. Cut the weed-control membrane or black polythene to fit the area to be gravelled, then lay it over the soil, tucking the edges in against the boards. Spread the gravel over it and put the two pots in place.

Front of house – shady

~

DESIGNER

Thomasina Tarling

It has to be said that, in terms of domestic architecture, the last fifty years have not been exactly a golden age. Many of us live in small semis or terraced houses with fronts that are stark and frankly boring to look at – not helped by the fact that so few houses built since the last war have windowsills large enough to take a windowbox. And there is no doubt that a few plants can transform the front of a house completely – when you do see one with lovely hanging baskets by the front door, and even plants climbing up the brickwork, it really gladdens the eye.

Our small 1960s semi also faced north, so was in shade for the best part of the day – an ideal candidate for brightening up. We opted for troughs upstairs and downstairs, fixed to the wall with stout brackets. We needed two 1.2m (4 ft) troughs under each window, but these troughs come in several different lengths, so obviously you should measure your own window and work out which combination of sizes will work best for you. Unless you find that the troughs are the exact same width as the windows, it looks better to have them a bit wider than a bit narrower. In the sundries list below I have given 4 × 1.2 m (4 ft) windowboxes as an example, with the appropriate number of brackets and so on for that size. Since the troughs filled with plants and compost will be quite heavy you'll need one bracket every 30 cm (1 ft) or so. To brighten the porch we planted up a half-barrel in the corner, and to twine round the post supporting the porch on the garden side we chose a scented semi-evergreen honeysuckle.

We wanted the house to look good all through the year, so we opted for mainly evergreen plants, with a fair proportion of golden foliage which really does brighten up a shady spot, and planned to ring the changes seasonally with a few bedding plants – one scheme in gold and white for summer and another in blue, gold and white to be planted in the autumn, for winter and spring. All the plants chosen will thrive in shade.

At its best all year round.

The front of this small modern house seems so much more welcoming now with its bright, colourful troughs.

—— *Plants* ——

FOR THE TROUGHS

4 Juniper (*Juniperus communis* 'Compressa')
Height/spread after 10 years: 60 × 15 cm (2 ft × 6 in)

4 Shrubby honeysuckle (*Lonicera nitida* 'Baggesen's Gold')
Height/spread after 10 years: 1.2 × 1.8 m (4 × 6 ft)

4 *Euonymus fortunei* 'Emerald 'n' Gold'
Height/spread after 10 years: 60 cm × 1 m (2 × 3 ft)

2 large Ivy (*Hedera helix* 'Buttercup' or 'Goldheart')
Height/spread after 10 years: 2.4 × 2.4 m (8 × 8 ft)

6 small Ivy (*Hedera helix* e.g. 'Parsley Crested' or 'Green Ripple')
Height/spread after 10 years: 1.2 m × 60 cm (4 × 2 ft)

2 *Heuchera micrantha* 'Palace Purple'
Height/spread: 60 × 50 cm (2 ft × 20 in)

FOR SUMMER

8 *Bidens aurea*
16 white *Impatiens* (busy Lizzie)

FOR WINTER

12 white universal pansies or polyanthus
12 blue universal pansies or polyanthus
48 *Narcissus* 'February Gold'

FOR THE BARREL

1 large *Camellia* 'Alba Simplex'
Height/spread after 10 years: 1.5 × 1.5 m (5 × 5 ft)

3 Creeping Jenny (*Lysimachia nummularia*)
Height/spread: 5 × 60 cm (2 in × 2 ft)

1 *Heuchera cylindrica* 'Greenfinch'
Height/spread: 60 × 50 cm (2 ft × 20 in)

N.B. Since all the above shrubs are restricted in containers, they will reach nothing like their full size; and, apart from the juniper and the camellia, they can all be clipped to keep them neat.

FOR THE POST

1 Honeysuckle (*Lonicera japonica* 'Aureoreticulata')
Height/spread after 10 years: 3 × 3 m (10 × 10 ft)

—— *Tools* ——

Hose or watering can
Electric drill
Masonry bit
Screwdriver

Trowel
Scissors
Stout gloves

—— Sundries ——

Half-barrel 50 cm (20 in) in
  diameter
4 1.2 m (4 ft) dark green plastic
  troughs
16 fixing brackets
48 5 cm (2 in) screws and
  rawlplugs
1 m (3 ft) stout plastic-coated wire
1.8 × 30 cm (6 × 1 ft) piece
  chicken wire
Garden twine

80 litres soil-based compost
25 litres ericaceous compost (for
  the camellia)
1 packet water-retaining gel
  crystals
16 Osmacote slow-release
  fertilizer plugs
2 disposable cleaning cloths
Broken polystyrene plant trays or
  packaging (for crocking the
  barrel and troughs)

—— Time ——

It should take about 3 hours: about 1½ hours to fix the brackets to the walls
and about 1–1½ hours to do the planting.

—— Method ——

1. Give all the plants a thorough watering.

2. Fix the brackets to the house walls, so that they are evenly spaced and the
top of the troughs will be about 7.5–10 cm (3–4 in) below the window –
much lower than that and they'll look odd; much higher and you'll clobber
the plants each time you open the windows.

3. Push out the indented drainage holes in the bottom of the troughs. Then
cut each cleaning cloth in two and lay one strip in the bottom of each
trough. This will allow the water to drain out, but will keep the compost
in, as the last thing you want, especially under the bedroom windows, is
dark brown, composty water dripping down the brickwork.

4. Part-fill the troughs with soil-based compost and mix in some water-
retaining gel crystals. These can hold many many times their own weight
in water and will stop the compost drying out too fast. Put the permanent
plants in the troughs, making sure that they are properly spaced and you've
got their best side to the front. In this instance put the tallest plants – the

junipers – right at the ends of the troughs so that you can open the windows pretty wide without touching them. Plant the bedding in the gaps and then fill in around them with compost, leaving a good 3–4 cm (1¼–1½ in) gap at the top so that you water without splashing. Push four plugs of slow-release fertilizer into each trough, spacing them evenly.

5. Put the troughs in place on the walls *before* you water. They'll be heavy enough as it is, even with two people to carry them.

6. Once the top troughs are in place, take the length of stout wire, and bend it into a loop. Then bend about 5 cm (2 in) of the two ends almost back on themselves. Hook one end over the front of one trough by the ivy

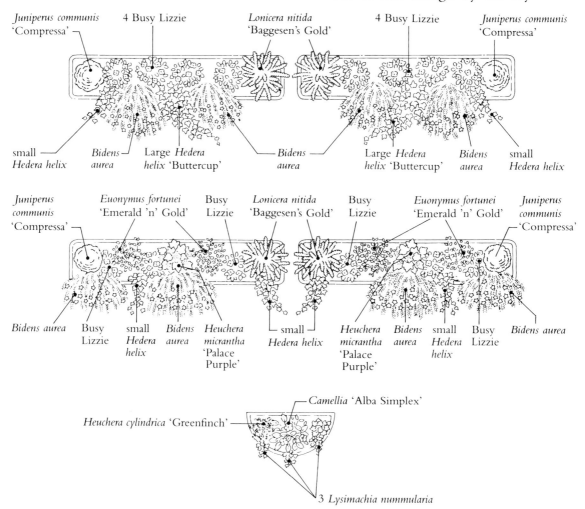

'Buttercup' or 'Goldheart' and hook the other end over the other trough in the same place, then wind the ivies round the wire so that eventually they will join up in the centre and form a swag.

7. Put the barrel in position before you start planting since it will be quite heavy to move afterwards. Place a layer of broken-up polystyrene in the bottom of the barrel and fill with ericaceous compost (this is for plants like camellias that must have a lime-free soil). Then plant in the usual way (see page 117).

8. Since twining plants like honeysuckle can't grow up something smooth like a metal post, take the piece of chicken wire (wearing gloves, since the cut ends can scratch) and wrap it loosely round the post. Then fasten it by bending the cut ends round other loops of the wire, making sure that the ends themselves finish up on the inside, not the outside. Plant the honeysuckle in the bed close to the post. It will need a bit of help to get started, so tie the stems to the wire with garden twine. Once it gets going, it should largely take care of itself, though you'll need to tuck the odd stray stem in.

9. If you want to keep the bidens over the winter, remove them before the first frosts and pot them up. In autumn, replace the summer bedding with the winter-flowering pansies or polyanthus, and dwarf daffodils.

The soft silvers, mauves and pinks of the planting here work well to soften the rather harsh red of the bricks.

Front of house – sunny

~

DESIGNER

Thomasina Tarling

This is a scheme for a modern house similar to the one in the project on page 94, only facing south or west this time, where sun-loving plants will thrive. Since the bathroom window of this house seemed more prominent, we put a trough under that one too, with the same planting as the double trough under the bedroom window.

Again the containers are designed to look attractive all the year with a good framework of evergreens, and the opportunity to add some seasonal bedding to change the colour scheme if you choose to.

At its best all year round, though the tub will be prettiest from mid- to late summer when the clematis is flowering.

—— *Time* ——

It should take two people 2–3 hours: about 1–1½ hours to fix the brackets to the walls and about 1–1½ hours to do the planting.

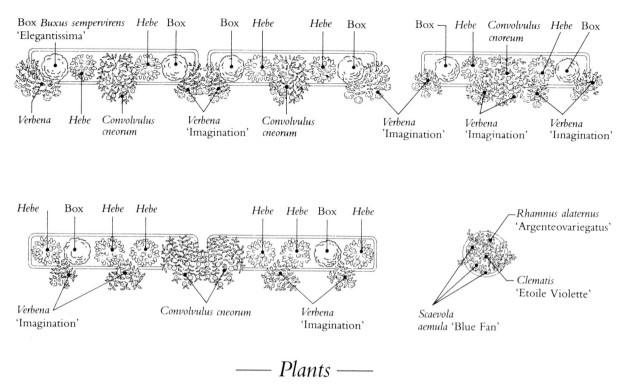

Box *Buxus sempervirens* 'Elegantissima'   *Hebe*   Box   Box   *Hebe*   *Hebe*   Box   Box   *Hebe*   *Convolvulus cnoreum*   *Hebe*   Box

Verbena   *Hebe*   *Convolvulus cneorum*   *Verbena* 'Imagination'   *Convolvulus cneorum*   *Verbena* 'Imagination'   *Verbena* 'Imagination'   *Verbena* 'Imagination'

Hebe   Box   *Hebe*   *Hebe*   *Hebe*   *Hebe*   Box   *Hebe*   *Rhamnus alaternus* 'Argenteovariegatus'

Verbena 'Imagination'   *Convolvulus cneorum*   *Verbena* 'Imagination'   *Clematis* 'Etoile Violette'

Scaevola aemula 'Blue Fan'

— Plants —

FOR THE TROUGHS

8 Box (*Buxus sempervirens* 'Elegantissima')
to be kept clipped at about 25–30 cm (10 in–1 ft)

5 *Convolvulus cneorum*
Height/spread after 10 years: 50 × 80 cm (20 in × 2½ ft)

6 *Hebe* 'Paula' (or any small, mauve-flowered hebe)
Height/spread: 30 × 60 cm (1 × 2 ft)

6 *Hebe* 'Baby Marie' (or any small, pink-flowered hebe)
Height/spread: 30 × 60 cm (1 × 2 ft)

18 *Verbena* 'Imagination'
Height/spread: 60 × 30 cm (2 × 1 ft)

FOR WINTER

10 pink cyclamen
(or 10 winter-flowering pansies in wine red)

FOR THE POT

1 *Clematis* 'Etoile Violette'
Height (in one season – you cut it back hard after flowering each year): 2.4 m (8 ft)

1 Italian buckthorn (*Rhamnus alaternus* 'Argenteovariegatus')
Height/spread: 2 × 1 m (6½ × 3 ft)

3 *Scaevola aemula* 'Blue Fan'
Height/spread: 30 × 60 cm (1 × 2 ft)

FOR WINTER

6 blue winter-flowering pansies

Sundries

1 terracotta pot 50 cm (20 in) in diameter

5 1.2 m (4 ft) dark green plastic troughs

20 fixing brackets

60 5 cm (2 in) screws and rawlplugs

Garden twine

80 litres soil-based compost

1 packet Erin water-retaining gel crystals

20 Osmacote slow-release fertilizer plugs

3 disposable cleaning cloths

Broken polystyrene plant trays or packaging (for crocking the pot and the troughs)

Tools

Hose or watering can

Electric drill

Masonry bit

Screwdriver

Trowel

Scissors

Method

1. Fix and plant up the troughs as described on page 95, but according to the plan for this project.

2. For the barrel, plant the rhamnus first, then plant the clematis behind it, so that its roots are sheltered from the sun, and train the growth around to the front. The scaevola is a half-hardy so don't plant it out until the end of May/ early June.

3. Once the clematis has finished flowering in autumn and the leaves have died, cut it back hard to about 15 cm (6 in) from the top of the compost. It will produce new growth again in the spring, and you don't want dead leaves spoiling the evergreen foliage of the rhamnus in winter. Before the first frosts take out the scaevolas and if you have a frost-free porch, or better still access to a greenhouse, you can pot them up and keep them over the winter. Put in the winter-flowering pansies. Replace the verbenas with cyclamen or pansies.

Instant height

~

DESIGNER

Jean Goldberry

One of the things that makes gardens and indeed borders much more interesting is changes of level. Taking the eye up and down, rather than simply along, makes it travel further and creates the impression that a space is larger than it really is. Lots of borders, especially newly planted ones, lack height. One solution is to use small trees or large shrubs, but of course it takes quite a long time for them to reach the height you want and then, in most cases, they don't just stop but keep on growing.

A simple way to provide instant height in a border is with a structure up which you can train fast-growing climbers such as clematis, honeysuckle, golden hop or solanum, or a mixture of plants, like a climbing rose with a clematis, or even two different varieties which flower at different times of the year, growing through it. The structure itself will provide impact while the plants are growing and, of course, it will never get any bigger.

There are some very good devices on the market now, like Whitchester Wood's 'Cocoon' which costs around £20. You hammer the stout wooden spike into the ground to a depth of about 45 cm (18 in) and then assemble the struts around it. The wood is treated so that it won't rot, but you could stain it with a wood stain in an attractive colour – blue, green, even red or yellow – to provide a foil for whatever you've chosen to plant.

A simple alternative would be to make a tripod from long round tree stakes with pointed ends that you wire together at the top to make a neat conical finish, and grow plants up that. In our garden, to balance the height of the tripod, we made the bed a little wider – about 1 m (3 ft) as opposed to 60 cm (2 ft) – and chose to grow up it the white-flowered relative of the Chilean potato vine (*Solanum jasminoïdes* 'Album'). The soil was a mixture of stones and clay, so we added organic matter to it for the plant. For once clay was an advantage here because it would hold the poles very firmly once they were in.

At its best in summer when the solanum is in flower, but it's semi-evergreen so you should get some winter greenery too.

This simple tripod, with *Solanum jasminoïdes* 'Album' growing up it, makes a strong, eye-catching feature in this otherwise flat border.

—— Plants ——

1 *Solanum jasminoïdes* 'Album'
Height/spread after 10 years: 3.7 × 3.7 m
(12 × 12 ft)

—— Sundries ——

Soil improver
Pelleted chicken manure or slow-release fertilizer
3 2.4 m (8 ft) Tannalized round tree stakes, 75 mm (3 in) in diameter, with pointed ends
6 galvanized staples
1 m (3 ft) stout garden wire

—— Tools ——

Hose or watering can
Spade
Fork
Hammer
Pegs
Pliers/wire cutters
Crowbar
Step ladder

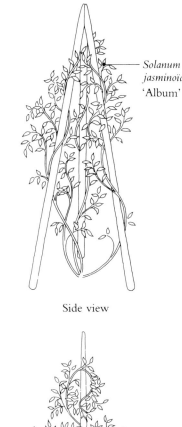

Solanum jasminoïdes 'Album'

Side view

Aerial view

—— Time ——

It should take two people about 2 hours; although it really does need two pairs of hands, you could do it on your own in 3–4 hours.

—— Method ——

1. Give all the plants a thorough watering.

2. Dig over the ground, improving the soil as necessary (see page 116).

3. Lay the posts out on the ground and fiddle with the pointed ends until you find the neatest arrangement. Then hammer in two staples on the outside of each point, one on each face, about 10 cm (4 in) from the top.

4. Decide which is the best arrangement for the tripod – two legs at the back and one at the front or vice versa – and use pegs to mark the positions for the holes, which should be about 60 cm (2 ft) apart and 30 cm (1 ft) deep. A tripod is naturally a very strong structure, so the poles don't need to be any deeper in the ground than that.

5. Dig the hole for the plant in the centre of the tripod.

6. The easiest way to make the holes for the three poles is to use the crowbar and a hammer to make the initial hole, then move the crowbar in ever increasing circles to make it wider and wider.

7. Put the poles in the holes and pull them together to make sure that they are all at the same height. If one is higher than the other two, make the relevant hole a bit deeper. If one is shorter than the other two, put a bit of soil in the bottom of that hole.

8. When the poles are in and level, loop the garden wire through the six staples around the top twice. Pull it as tight as you can by hand, then twist the ends together, cut off the excess and, with the pliers, twist the ends round and round to take up any slack. (Depending on how tall you are, you may need to use the step ladder to reach the top.)

9. Plant the climber in the usual way (see page 119).

10. Fill in the holes around the poles with soil and hammer it down to hold them firmly in place. You'll find it really does make them rock-steady.

11. Train the stems of the climber around all three legs of the tripod.

Mini rose garden

~

DESIGNER

Penelope Smith

To many people 'rose garden' conjures up a huge stately garden or a public park, with beds full of hybrid teas planted *en masse* in soldierly rows – colourful when they're in flower in summer, but stark and angular for the rest of the time. New developments in rose breeding mean that many roses are now available that make much more attractive plants without sacrificing their free-flowering qualities, and, with some judicious underplanting, can make a very eye-catching feature.

Our garden had just had a brand-new fence 1.2 m (4 ft) high, with what had once been a semi-circular bed but which was now overgrown with weeds. The soil was on the heavy side, and so the drainage needed improving with grit and organic matter, and it faced south. We decided on an assortment of roses of different habits and sizes. First there's 'Mary Rose', one of the New English roses bred by David Austin to have all the scent and beauty of old varieties but with modern vigour and disease-resistance. This one has rich deep pink flowers. Then we chose one of the new 'County' series of ground-cover roses, the lovely, white, low-growing 'Kent', with an old favourite, the tall, arching *Rosa glauca*, grown primarily for its wonderful, smoky, purply-grey foliage, at the back. It does have flowers too, single ones in a similar rich pink to 'Mary Rose'. We underplanted with lavender to give year-round structure to the border, though hardy geraniums, like 'Johnson's Blue', and violas in blues or white, or even pale yellow, if it tones with the colour of the roses, would also be an excellent choice.

At its best from May to October.

By next summer, the roses and lavender will have started to fill their allotted space.

—— *Plants* ——

1 Rose (*Rosa glauca*)
Height/spread after 10 years: 2.4 × 1.8 m
(8 × 6 ft)

2 Rose (*Rosa* 'Mary Rose')
Height/spread after 10 years: 1.2 × 1.2 m
(4 × 4 ft)

3 Rose (*Rosa* 'Kent')
Height/spread after 10 years: 45 × 60 cm
(18 in × 2 ft)

5 Lavender (*Lavandula angustifolia* 'Munstead')
Height/spread after 10 years: 45 × 45 cm
(18 in × 18 in)

—— *Sundries* ——

Soil improver
Pelleted chicken manure or slow-release fertilizer
***2* 120 litre sacks of cocoa shells**

—— *Tools* ——

Hose or watering can
Spade
Fork
Tape measure
Rope (washing line or hose will do) *or* measuring line (a length of string with a wooden peg at each end will do) and pegs or skewers
Wheelbarrow or groundsheet

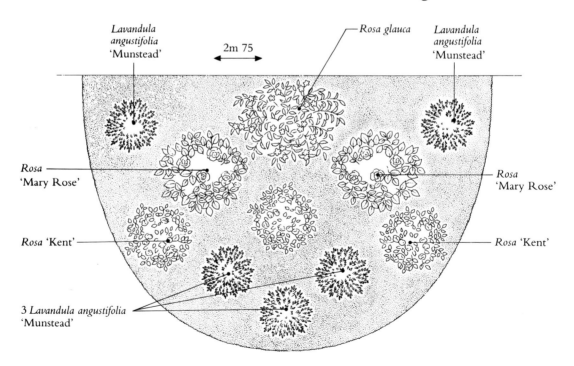

Lavandula angustifolia 'Munstead'

2m 75

Rosa glauca

Lavandula angustifolia 'Munstead'

Rosa 'Mary Rose'

Rosa 'Mary Rose'

Rosa 'Kent'

Rosa 'Kent'

3 *Lavandula angustifolia* 'Munstead'

—— *Time* ——

It should take two people 2–3 hours; one person 3–4 hours. Digging out the bed is by far the longest job.

—— *Method* ——

1. Give all the plants a thorough watering.

2. Mark out and dig the semi-circular bed in the same way as you would for 'Disguising a fence', steps 2–3 (see page 73). Improve the soil as necessary (see page 116).

3. Set all the roses out in their pots, and make any adjustments then. Plant them in the usual way (see page 117). Then interplant the lavenders, weaving them through the roses.

4. Water well and spread with a layer of cocoa shells.

Barrels of fun

~

DESIGNER

Penelope Smith

Barrels – or, to be more accurate, half-barrels – make excellent containers in the garden because they are big and chunky and, compared to other containers, quite cheap, so you get a lot of pot for your money. They are ideal for permanent planting – for growing shrubs or even small trees – and a group of them can transform a dull spot on a patio or in a corner.

Our site was a brick wall alongside a patio, overhung by large trees, so it was in shade for much of the day. We decided to opt for foliage, not flowers, and for a Japanese feel, so we chose just three plants – bamboo (*Fargesia murieliae*), a wine-red Japanese maple (*Acer palmatum* 'Dissectum Atropurpureum') and a very low-growing juniper. These gave us three strongly contrasting shapes – the tall thin bamboo, the umbrella-shaped maple and the very strong horizontal line of the juniper. We planted them in three barrels, one large, two slightly smaller, and since it was such a shady spot we painted them with a pale grey architectural wood stain which added some lightness but which at the same time, being such a neutral shade, didn't detract from the foliage colour. Incidentally, once they are full of plants and compost they are very heavy indeed, so get them in the right position before you plant them up. Because the maple prefers an acid soil, we used a special lime-free (ericaceous) compost in that barrel.

At its best from late spring to autumn, though good all year.

A simple contrast in shapes – horizontal, vertical and arching – livens up this shady wall, and the fact that they are in containers means they'll never get too big.

Plants

1 Japanese maple (*Acer palmatum* 'Dissectum Atropurpureum')
Height/spread after 10 years: 1.2 × 1.5 m (4 × 5 ft)

1 Bamboo (*Fargesia murieliae*) (still often sold as *Arundinaria murieliae*)
Height/spread after 10 years: 4 m (13 ft) × infinite

1 Juniper (*Juniperus communis* 'Repanda')
Height/spread after 10 years: 25 cm × 1.2 m (10 in × 4 ft)

Sundries

1 **half-barrel 50 cm (20 in) in diameter**
2 **half-barrels 38 cm (15 in) in diameter**
1 **250 ml tin pale grey wood stain**
White spirit
2 **broken polystyrene plant trays or packaging (for crocking)**
80 litres soil-based compost
25 litres ericaceous compost (for the acer)
12 **Slow-release fertilizer plugs**

Tools

Hose or watering can
Stiff bristle or wire brush
Paint brush
Trowel

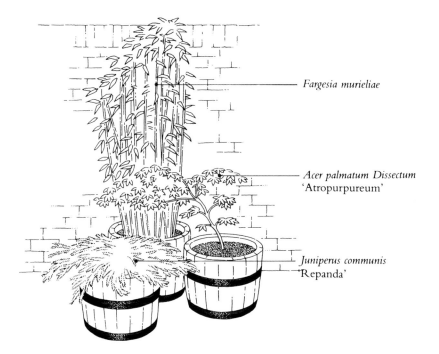

Fargesia murieliae

Acer palmatum Dissectum 'Atropurpureum'

Juniperus communis 'Repanda'

—— Time ——

It should take two people about 2 hours, one person about 3 hours, though you'll need to allow the wood finish to dry between coats.

—— Method ——

1. Brush the half-barrels over with a good stiff brush to remove any debris, then paint them. Leave the first coat to dry thoroughly, then put on the second coat.

2. Give the plants a thorough soaking.

3. When the barrels are completely dry, put the plants inside them, still in their pots, and position them in the most visually appealing arrangement. Then take the plants out again, place a shallow layer of broken-up polystyrene in the bottom, followed by some compost, and plant in the usual way, leaving a good 3–4 cm (1¼–1½ in) at the top so that you can water easily without splashing.

4. Push four fertilizer plugs per barrel into the compost, evenly spaced.

Techniques

What does it all mean?

Lots of new gardeners are rather put off by the vocabulary of gardening, and understandably so. I'm the same with cars, I only have to hear terms like 'overhead camshaft' and my eyes glaze over. But, like all technical terms, they are a very useful shorthand, so here are a few basic terms explained.

A **shrub** is a bush with lots of woody stems. It can be evergreen and keep its leaves all year or it can be deciduous and lose its leaves in winter, but its woody stems remain.

A **perennial** is a plant that usually dies back in the winter, leaving no woody stems above ground, but produces new growth in the spring every year. There are some evergreen perennials, like lambs' lugs and hellebores, but their stems are always soft, not woody like a shrub's.

A **half-hardy** or **tender perennial** is a plant from a hot climate, such as a pelargonium (what most people call 'geranium') or an osteospermum, which is usually killed off by frost in winter in this country. It will sometimes survive the winter in a very sheltered garden or inside in a greenhouse or frost-free porch.

An **alpine**, technically speaking, is a plant from mountain regions, but the term has come to be used for a whole range of small low-growing plants, including Mediterranean herbs like thyme, which all like the same growing conditions – a very gritty, open, free-draining soil and, in most instances, a sunny spot.

An **annual** is a plant that is grown from seed, flowers and dies within one summer. Many of them self-seed, which means they drop their seeds in the soil around them. Those seeds then lie dormant during the winter but germinate in spring and produce new plants for that summer. All you have to do in subsequent years is hoe or pull out the plants where you don't want them.

Soil improver is some form of bulky, well-rotted, organic substance – garden compost, well-rotted farmyard manure, spent hops, composted bark, green waste – which improves the water-retaining abilities of the soil. Most soil improvers contain some nutrients, but unless you are working on soil that has been well managed over the years, you'll need additional nutrients – fertilizers – as well.

Fertilizers are either organic – bonemeal, hoof and horn, blood, fish and bone, pelleted chicken manure – or inorganic – rose fertilizer, Growmore (not a brand name, incidentally, but a formula), pelleted fertilizer like Osmacote. Some fertilizers are quick-release (chicken manure, for example, and blood, fish and bone) to get the plants off to a flying start, while the others are slow-release. If you add some of each type when you're planting you don't have to worry about feeding again in the first season.

Use all fertilizers strictly at the rate recommended on the packet. In this instance 'a bit more for good luck' will either be a waste of money or could actually do the plants harm.

A **mulch** is a layer you put on top of the soil after planting to keep weeds down and moisture in. You can use 7.5–10 cm (3–4 in) of coarse bark, cocoa shells, shredded prunings, gravel, or a special water-permeable planting membrane like Plantex or even black polythene, although with the two latter you need a very thin layer of something more attractive to look at on top. Since one aim of mulching is to keep moisture in, make sure that you water the bed thoroughly before you put it on.

Your soil

Now I realize that for many beginners the mention of 'soil' and the need to know just a little bit about it is a huge turn-off, but I can't stress how important it is if you want to grow plants successfully. If you try to grow something in the wrong type of soil, it will never thrive and may well die, and that's very dispiriting. So please, don't skip this bit!

As I said in the introduction, all the projects in

the book use plants that will do well in an average soil – soil that isn't too heavy and wet, nor too free-draining and dry, not too acid, nor too alkaline. So for example, there are no bog plants, nor are there any acid-lovers like rhododendrons or camellias (except in containers where you can give them exactly the kind of compost they like). But if you have a heavy clay soil or a very poor, dry one, you will need to improve it before you start to plant anything. Of course, you could do nothing to the soil and just plant shrubs and perennials that will cope with the conditions, but that will mean you have an extremely limited range of plants to choose from, and there's very, very little that won't grow much better in slightly improved conditions. Besides, all these projects are on a very small scale – only a few square metres in most instances – so the prospect isn't as daunting as it might be if you were tackling the whole garden.

Knowing your soil type

The easiest and certainly the best way to start learning about your soil is to pick it up and handle it. If it feels sticky and you can mould it easily into a ball when it's wet, or if it's baked like concrete when it's dry, you have a heavy clay soil. If it feels silky between your fingers, you have a silt soil which has many of the same problems as clay and needs to be improved in much the same way. If it feels very gritty and won't hold together in a ball no matter how hard you squeeze, you have a sandy soil. If your soil looks dry, greyish and crumbly and contains a lot of stones, flints and even pieces of white chalk, that's what you're gardening on – chalk. Most soils, of course, are a mixture of these various extreme types, but even so it should be pretty obvious from the feel of it which type you have.

If you have drawn first prize in the horticultural lottery of life you will have a medium loam – a rich, dark brown soil that retains moisture but is never waterlogged, and is so fertile that you daren't stand still for too long or else your feet will grow roots! It must be said, though, that, as in life, very, very few of us do win first prize, but the good news is that you

can almost certainly improve your soil as much as is necessary for most of the plants we're using to grow very well.

Acid or limy?

Although none of the plants (with the exception of the odd one in a container) we're using in these projects must have either an acid or very limy soil, it is still well worth finding out at the beginning whether your soil is acid or limy – what its pH is – because, without being too dramatic about it, the amount of lime in the soil is a matter of life or death for some plants. Rhododendrons and summer-flowering heathers, for example, are lime haters and on an alkaline soil they will simply die.

Lime-testing kits are available from all garden centres, cost about £1 and are very easy to use. What you do is take several small samples of your soil from about 10 cm (4 in) down from different parts of the garden (you may find quite surprising variations within the garden), put them on separate saucers and leave them to dry out. Then put one sample at a time in the test tube provided, add the chemical and top up with distilled water. Don't use tap water – its own pH varies from area to area and could affect your result.

Shake the test tube, then leave it for a while. Eventually the soil settles at the bottom of the tube and you are left with a coloured liquid on the top, which you compare with the colours on the chart provided. Don't expect the colour of the liquid to be as bright and clear-cut as the ones on the chart, though – it'll be a much sludgier version of those colours! Roughly speaking, the more orange the colour of the liquid, the lower the pH and the more acid your soil. Neutral soil, with a pH of 7, is a mid-green, and dark green liquid indicates an alkaline soil. If yours is a neutral-to-acid soil, you can grow almost all ornamental plants with ease.

Improving your soil

The ideal soil for all these projects is one that is free-draining, but at the same time doesn't lose moisture and nutrients too quickly. The few that need a very free-draining soil require additional grit digging in. What you need to do to make your soil as close to ideal as possible depends, of course, on what you start with.

Clay

Clay is without doubt the most difficult soil, initially anyway, because when it's wet, it's a sticky boggy morass, and when it's dry, it's as hard as concrete, and neither of these states is exactly hospitable to plants or to gardeners' backs. That's the bad news. The good news is that, with work, a clay soil will grow far better plants than a very light, sandy soil ever can. If your soil is really heavy and wet, you may have to install a drainage system, but fortunately that's an extreme situation and you're unlikely to be that unlucky.

The best way to improve an averagely sticky clay or silt soil is to start by double-digging it – digging a trench to one spade's depth, then breaking up the soil in the bottom of the trench to another spade's depth with a fork and working in both coarse grit – about one barrowload to every 3 sq m (33 sq ft) or one and a half bucketfuls to every 1 sq m (11 sq ft) – and the same amount of organic matter. The grit will open up the soil and allow air and water to pass more freely through it. The organic matter helps to open up the soil too, but in the case of well-made garden compost or well-rotted (and it must be well-rotted) animal manure it also helps retain moisture and contains nutrients too. If you live in a town or city, look in your local Yellow Pages under 'Garden Services' or even 'Riding Stables' for a supplier.

If you don't have any garden compost or a ready source of animal manure, there are all sorts of alternatives available now from garden centres at a price – composted bark, de-limed mushroom compost, spent hops, recycled green waste (often the shredded prunings of trees and shrubs, composted down). In this instance you don't want a concentrated manure since bulk is what you need.

Make sure that the grit and compost are well mixed into all levels of the soil. The easiest way of doing this is to fork some grit and compost into the

soil at the bottom of each trench, half-fill it with some of the soil you've dug out, spread another layer of grit and compost, then refill the trench completely with soil.

By adding all this organic matter and grit to the soil, you are raising the soil level a bit, which will also help it to drain more freely.

You will make life much easier for yourself if you can dig heavy clay soil when it is neither dry and hard as a rock nor thoroughly waterlogged and you're knee-deep in mud – ideally when it's drying out but still moist. Probably the best time is autumn so that, having dug it over roughly, you can leave it for the winter frosts to work on. As it dries out, the large lumps crack, and when water gets into those cracks and freezes, it forces them wider apart, breaking the soil down into smaller and smaller clods. With a bit of luck and a few good hard frosts, you'll find that in the spring you need only rake it down.

If the soil is like a pudding when you want to plant, you really have no choice but to leave it until it's dried out a bit. You should *never* walk on a heavy soil when it is wet, since you are simply compounding the problem. If, for some reason, you simply have to walk on it, always put down wide scaffolding planks to spread the weight. If it's very dry and hard and you are absolutely determined to get on, you can break up the surface with a pick. Desperate situations call for desperate remedies, but because clay soils hold the moisture well, you could find that the soil is quite moist a few centimetres below the surface and so, once the surface is broken, it's possible to dig the rest over.

Sand

At first glance, compared to heavy clay soils, sandy soils are a piece of cake to cultivate. Because they are so free-draining, they are workable when clay and silt are still waterlogged, they warm up quickly in spring and are very easy to dig over in preparation for planting. The downside with sandy soils is that they dry out very quickly, losing not just moisture but valuable plant nutrients too. For that reason they need large amounts of organic matter to help retain moisture, and plant nutrients in the form of fertilizers every year. But since organic matter will work its way through the thin topsoil very quickly and into the subsoil, it is a waste of time – and compost – to dig it in too deeply. Either dig it in to the top few centimetres of soil only or just spread it over the surface and allow the elements and the worms to work it in for you. Since sandy soils lose moisture through surface evaporation as well as through free drainage, spreading a layer of organic matter on the surface helps keep the moisture in too.

Chalk

Chalky soils share many of the same advantages and problems as sand. They are very free-draining and are rarely too wet to work, but they lose water and nutrients very rapidly. They have an additional problem in that the layer of topsoil is usually shallow and very limy, which limits the range of plants that will grow happily. The way to improve it is much the same as with sand – add lots of organic matter and fertilizer, and keep the surface of the soil covered as far as you can, to retain moisture. If you can use acid organic matter, like well-rotted manure, garden compost or cocoa shells, for digging in and mulching, that'll help to counteract the alkalinity of the soil, but only to a small degree. You certainly won't make it acid enough to grow lime-hating plants.

Medium loam

If you are lucky enough to have medium loam, it won't need much work to improve it, but it's still worth working in some organic matter when you dig it over to get the plants off to a flying start.

Planting techniques

Watering before you plant

The first thing to do when starting any of the projects in this book is to give all the plants a thorough soaking while they are still in their pots. That way it's much easier to guarantee that the root ball is thoroughly moist than it is by watering once the plants are in the soil. It also makes it much easier to slip them out of the pots when you're ready to plant. Water them with a watering can or hose till the water starts coming out of the bottom of the pot *and* it feels much heavier to lift than it did before you started. The second part is very important because sometimes, if the plants are very dry, the compost will have shrunk away from the sides of the pot, so water starts pouring out long before the compost is wet through. With smaller plants a foolproof method is to plunge the pots into a bucket of water and hold them – the pots, that is, not the plants – just under the surface until air bubbles stop rising from the compost. Then leave them to drain. By the time you're ready to put them in, they should be just right.

Trees and shrubs

Having dug over the area you're going to plant up, you're ready to dig the first hole, and it makes sense to plant the largest shrubs or trees first. You might wonder, since you're going to be digging all these planting holes, why you need bother to dig the whole bed over first. Why not just dig the holes, bung in a bit of compost and fertilizer and plant straight into that? I'll tell you why. If you simply dig a hole in uncultivated ground, particularly on a clay soil, the hole will act as a sump, drawing water in from the land around, so what you'd be doing is planting your tree or shrub in cold waterlogged soil. If you're lucky, the plant will just be very slow to start into growth. If you're unlucky, the roots will either be deprived of air and drown or will rot away and your tree or shrub will die.

Dig a hole three or four inches deeper and wider than the container, then mix a little soil with some compost and put it in the bottom of the hole with some fertilizer – either pelleted chicken manure or a slow-release granular fertilizer. Check that it is the right depth by putting the container in the hole, then laying a bamboo cane or even your spade across it. If the cane rests on the soil on both sides *and* the top of the container, the hole is deep enough. Take the tree or shrub carefully out of its pot. If it's a rigid plastic pot and you've watered it thoroughly beforehand, it should lift out fairly easily. If it doesn't, try gently squeezing the sides of the pot just to loosen the soil. If all else fails, you'll have to cut the pot away, using a Stanley knife or something similar.

If the roots are wound round and round in a tight circle, gently tease them out – with the emphasis on 'gently' – so that they can start growing quickly out into the surrounding soil. Some shrubs will be all right if you don't do this, although they'll be a bit slower to take off, while others, like conifers, will suffer. Their roots will continue to grow round and round, which makes them very unstable once they've been planted and likely to blow over in a gale.

Put the root ball into the hole and make sure that the tree or shrub is facing the right way – in other words, with its best side to the front. Spread out the loosened roots carefully and start to shovel in the soil. When you've half-filled the hole, firm the soil a little with the ball of your foot. The aim is to get rid of any large air pockets and help the soil come into close contact with the roots but not to compress it too much and make it airless, or damage any fine roots, so go gently. Fill in the rest of the hole and gently firm the soil once more.

Staking

All new trees need staking, but recent research has shown that short stakes – reaching only one third of the way up the trunk – are more efficient than the traditional, much longer ones. Allowing the top of the tree to sway about in the wind thickens the base of the trunk and helps strengthen the root system. To work out the best length for a stake, measure the height of the tree's trunk and divide by three (to give one third its length), and add 45 cm (18 in) to go into the ground. Then hammer the stake diagonally into the soil behind the tree and close to the trunk.

Attach the stake to the trunk with a special

plastic tree tie which has a collar to prevent it chafing. Whatever you do, don't use wire or nylon twine, which will cut into the tree as it grows and either kill it or allow diseases in. If you're not too bothered about appearances, you can use an old nylon stocking tied in a figure of eight around the tree and the stake, but, to be honest, proper tree ties are so cheap it's really not worth the bother.

Climbers

You plant climbers in more or less the same way as you plant other shrubs, with just a couple of differences. Do bear in mind that the soil at the bottom of a fence or wall (and particularly a house wall, where the overhanging eaves keep most of the rain off it) is usually very dry. So always add lots of moisture-retaining organic matter to the planting hole and make sure that the stem of the climber itself at soil level is at least 30 cm (1 ft) away from the wall. Second, always plant clematis so that the top of the compost is at least 10 cm (4 in) *below* the surface of the soil. This is because most clematis, and particularly the large-flowered hybrids, are vulnerable to a disease called clematis wilt, which kills off the top growth very suddenly, right down to soil level. But it doesn't go below soil level, and by planting that bit lower you'll usually find that there are buds underneath the soil which can produce healthy new growth, so you don't lose the plant altogether. Spraying the new growth with benomyl or Bordeaux mixture will help prevent the disease striking again.

Supporting climbers

Whether or not climbers need supporting depends on which type they are. There are three main types. First there are the self-clingers like ivy, Virginia creeper and the climbing hydrangea, which have little suckers that cling on to the surface up which they're climbing. Ivy has had a very bad press because people think its roots damage brickwork, but as long as the pointing is sound the suckers do no harm at all.

With all self-clingers it's only the new growth that clings, so when they've just been planted, they'll need some help to get a grip. Leave them tied to the bamboo cane up which they're growing in the pot and push it towards the wall or fence. Or your could use those special self-sticking plastic ties in a few places, just to hold the growth against the hard surface until it starts to cling.

One very good gardener I know plants ivy by taking the stems off the cane and spreading them out horizontally along the ground with a bit of soil over them. That way they produce lots of vertical growths along the lengths of the stems and cover a wider expanse of wall or fence more quickly than ivies grown in the usual way.

Climbers and twiners, like honeysuckle, jasmine and clematis, which attach themselves by twining either their stems or their leaf stalks around something else do need support.

The cheapest method for fences is to stretch horizontal wires between the fence posts, starting with the lowest one about 60 cm (2 ft) from the ground and the rest above it about 30 cm (1 ft) apart, and secure them with staples. To make a mesh you then weave thinner wires vertically through them 30 cm (1 ft) apart and secure them on the top and bottom horizontal wires. Alternatively you can tack a piece of sheep wire (like chicken wire, only with a bigger mesh) over the whole fence, which gives complete coverage and allows the plants to grow in a very natural-looking way. Staple it on, top and bottom, and it's virtually invisible once it's in place.

As for the walls, you could fix wooden battens – 25 × 25 mm (about 1 in) square – to them first, using Rawlplugs and screws, and then attach wires to the battens in the same way as you would to a fence. This lifts the wires clear of the wall, not only allowing twiners to get behind them, but also letting air circulate and help prevent diseases like mildew on roses. Alternatively you could do what designer Jean Goldberry does and use wires, held in position by masonry nails with two washers slipped on to the end, to form a diamond grid, which both looks good and encourages the plants to grow diagonally, again giving more natural-looking coverage than if they were growing straight up and across. Obviously you need to make sure that the hole in the middle of the washers is small enough not to slip over the heads of the nails. What you do is hammer the nail almost home, wind the end of the wire round it *between* the two washers, then hammer it home so that the wire is gripped between the washers.

You could use wooden or plastic trellising, fixed to the fence posts or the battens on the walls, but it's more expensive and more obtrusive than wires.

Climbers in the third group, which includes roses and wall shrubs like pineapple broom (*Cytisus battandieri*), have no means of support, visible or otherwise, and so they do need to be tied in. Use one of the methods described for the second group and tie the plants to the wires or trellis using soft garden twine.

If you've got climbers that need support in only a few places (some climbing roses, for example), try lead-headed nails, which you simply hammer into the wall and then bend the attached flange round the stem of the plant. If you find, however, that you're having to bang in more and more nails, one of the other methods is preferable.

Perennials

The principles of planting perennials are really much the same as for other permanent ornamental plants. Prepare the ground well, then give the plants a really thorough soaking in their pots a few hours before you plant them.

It's always a good idea to place the plants in position, still in their pots, before you plant, so that you can play around with them, moving them about until they look right.

With bigger plants it pays dividends to dig a large hole — what that great Edwardian gardener Gertrude Jekyll used to call 'a half-crown hole for a sixpenny plant' — and fill it with good soil, mixed with compost and some fertilizer, and plant into that. For small plants, given that you will have prepared the whole bed very well, you should be able to make a small hole very easily with a trowel. Once your plants are in, firm the soil around them gently with your knuckles and then give them a thorough watering.

Caring for newly planted borders and containers

It is *absolutely essential* to keep newly-planted trees and shrubs well watered. It's a sad fact that over half of all trees and shrubs planted die within the first years, and there's no doubt that failure to give them enough water is the primary reason. Watering them thoroughly in their pots before you plant helps, and so does giving them another thorough soaking once they're in, but you really do need to water regularly and copiously throughout their first growing season.

Many gardeners, even quite experienced ones, can easily underestimate how much water plants need, and how long it takes to saturate the soil at the lower levels where it's really needed – where the roots are. If you wet just the surface, thirsty roots will come looking for water there, and will be even more susceptible to damage from hot sun or drying winds.

If you have only a watering can, I would strongly recommend that you buy a hose with a sprinkler, because in dry weather you need to leave the hose on for several hours – even overnight – for it to do any real good. Standing there holding the hose just isn't an option – even if you didn't get bored stiff after the first couple of hours, your hand would probably go numb! In a warm dry spell the odd shower can be a real curse, as you might be tempted to think that you don't need to bother to water. But unless the heavens have opened for an hour or two, you'll still need to do it!

Containers are particularly vulnerable because the plants form a very successful umbrella over the compost and the vast majority of raindrops just roll off the leaves and never make it through to the compost underneath. So it's probably safest to assume that you need to water them every day – twice a day when it's hot – even if it rains. Indeed the neighbours of the most successful roof gardener I've ever met think he is mad because they often see him out in the rain, umbrella in one hand, hosepipe in the other!

Bulbs

Bulbs are a first-class way to extend the flowering season, since they start blooming in early spring when there's very little else around. Although I haven't specifically included them in every project, it would be an excellent idea to plant some bulbs in among the shrubs and perennials wherever possible.

Spring-flowering bulbs – daffodils, crocuses, anemones – should be planted from September onwards, though tulips shouldn't be put in until November in case they start into growth too quickly and are nobbled by the frost. Lilies can be planted either in autumn or spring.

The one thing all bulbs hate is waterlogged soil – it rots them in no time – so if you have a heavy clay soil, having improved it, of course, to make it more free-draining, take the belt-and-braces approach and always plant them on a thick layer of coarse grit.

It's very important to plant all bulbs deeply enough. If they're planted too shallowly, they're likely to get too hot in summer and to be starved of moisture and either die or refuse to flower the following year. A quick rule of thumb for bulbs is to plant them at three times their own depth at least, so that they wind up with twice their own depth of soil on top of them. A bulb that's 2.5 cm (1 in) deep, for example, needs to be planted in a hole at least 7.5 cm (3 in) deep, so that the bulb has 5 cm (2 in) of soil on top of it.

You can plant large bulbs, like tulips or daffodils, individually using a bulb planter (get one with a soil-releasing mechanism, otherwise you can spend ages trying to get the plug of soil out of the planter!), or you can plant them in one large hole in a group. The latter is certainly the best method for small bulbs. In among shrubs and perennials, clumps or drifts of bulbs look much better than straight lines or single-tons dotted about the place, and *en masse* they make much more of an impact too.

If your bulbs are to remain permanently in your borders (and in a small garden, few people have the space or the inclination to lift them, dry them and store them), you need to plant them where they're unlikely to be disturbed. It's so easy, once all trace of them has disappeared in summer, to slice through them with the spade as you're digging away. So plant them close to shrubs and the middle of clumps of perennials where you're unlikely to be digging anyway. Planting bulbs with perennials also solves the problem of what to do with all that untidy bulb foliage once flowering's finished and before you can pull it out (roughly six weeks after the last flower has faded). If you're going to plant three cranesbills – *Geranium* 'Johnson's Blue', for instance – in an irregular triangle shape, fill the centre of that triangle with small bulbs like crocuses, *Anemone blanda* or squills. In winter and spring, when the bulbs are growing and in flower, all you can see of the cranesbills are small brown tufts. By the time the bulbs have finished flowering, the cranesbills have started into growth, and by the time the bulbs' foliage is beginning to die off, the cranesbills' new, fresh green leaves will hide it completely.

It's all too easy, too, to forget about feeding bulbs – out of sight, out of mind – but a handful or two of blood, fish and bone or a watering with a liquid fertilizer once flowering is over will pay dividends with next year's flowers.

As for colours, it's a good idea to choose bulbs to blend in with the colour scheme of the bed or border. In our shady island bed, for example (see page 63), with its evergreen foliage, gold, blue and white bulbs would be lovely, while with the smoky purples and silvers of the evergreen foliage in our semi-circular bed against the fence (see page 71) blue, white and pink would blend beautifully.

Suppliers and stockists

If you find it hard to find certain plants locally, it's well worth consulting *The Plant Finder* published yearly by the Royal Horticultural Society which lists over sixty thousand plants and nurseries which supply them, many of them via mail order. Buying from **reputable** nurseries this way is a very safe option (though you should beware of those small ads in newspapers offering 'Miracle' this or that) because the plants are packed with great care, the quality is high and if there is ever a problem with plants arriving damaged, the nursery will replace them free of charge. Do remember though that most plants bought mail order are sent out in autumn or late winter/early spring while they are dormant, and so many perennials and deciduous climbers like clematis will look dead when they arrive. Have faith, and plant them as soon as possible after they arrive, provided of course the ground is not frozen or waterlogged. In the spring your faith will be rewarded.

Hiding the shed
Trellis panels, posts and fittings are available from branches of Harcros Builders Merchants nationwide and other good builders' merchants.

Wood stain. Hicksons Decor 'Neptune' available from good builders' merchants or for your nearest stockist, contact Hicksons Timber Products Ltd., Sowgate Lane, Knottingley, W. Yorkshire WF11 0BS. Tel: 01977 671771.

Mini jungle
Chusan palm (*Trachycarpus fortunei*). Available by mail order from The Palm Centre, 563 Upper Richmond Road, London SW14 7ED. Tel: 0181 876 6888.

Bamboo (*Fargesia nitida*). Available from The Bamboo Centre at the same address as The Palm Centre (above).

Terra Perma pots, available from all good garden centres. Contact Richard Sankey on 01602 277335 for your nearest stockist.

Herb garden
Tegula cobbles by Marshalls. Available from all good garden centres and builders' merchants. For your nearest stockist contact Marshalls, Southowram, Halifax HX3 9SY. Tel: 01422 366666.

Mediterranean corner
Trifolium repens 'Wheatfen'. Available by mail order from PW Plants, Sunnyside, Heath Road, Kenninghall, Norfolk NR16 2DS. Tel: 01953 888212.

Echeveria elegans. Available by mail order from Bloomsbury, Upper Lodge Farm, Padworth Common, Reading, Berkshire. RG7 4JD. Tel: 01734 700239.

Flue liners. For your nearest stockist contact Redbank Manufacturing Ltd., Mesham, Swadlincote, Derbyshire. Tel: 01530 273737.

Shallow terracotta basket and 6-in high dish. From Barters Farm Nurseries, Chapmanslade, Westbury, Wiltshire. Tel: 01373 832294.

Water feature
Mini Cascade pump from Hozelock. Available at good garden centres. For your nearest stockist, contact Hozelock Ltd., Haddenham, Aylesbury, Buckinghamshire HP17 8JD. Tel: 01844 292002.

Plumberfix. Available from all builders' merchants.

Brightening up a patio
Pebbles. Arran Pebbles from Cempack. Available at good garden centres. For your nearest stockist, contact Cempack, Forge Lane, Thornhill, Dewsbury, W. Yorkshire WF12 9BU. Tel: 01924 452644.

Sitting pretty
6 ft rose arch with lattice infill from Agriframes. Available from good garden centres or direct from Agriframes, Charlwoods Road, East Grinstead, W. Sussex RH19 2HG. Tel: 01342 319111.

Alpine path

Heritage in 'Yorkstone' by Marshalls. Available from all good garden centres and builders' merchants. For your nearest stockist, contact Marshalls as above.

Front of house (shady and sunny)

Window boxes by Stewarts available from all good garden centres. For your nearest stockist contact The Stewart Company, Stewart House, Waddon March Way, Purley Way, Croydon CR9 4HS. Tel: 0181 686 2231.

Instant height

'Cocoon' from good garden centres or for your nearest stockist contact Whitchester Wood, The P&A Group of Companies, Mold Industrial Estate, Wrexham Road, Mold, Clwyd. Tel: 01352 752555.

Barrels of fun

Solignum Architectural Opaque Wood Stain in Arctic Grey. Available from good builders' merchants or for your nearest stockist contact Protim Solignum, Fieldhouse Lane, Marlow, Buckinghamshire SL7 1LS. Tel: 01628 486644.

Index